Learning to Love

at the School of John Paul II and Benedict XVI

"There have been many answers to the perennial question, 'What is love?'. In *Learning to Love at the School of John Paul II and Benedict XVI*, Mgr Livio Melina brings together the anthropology of Blessed John Paul II and the Augustinian wisdom of Pope Benedict XVI. Drawing on responsibility, the theology of the body and the truth of man and woman, he refutes Nietzsche's claim that Christianity poisoned eros. Setting aside both romanticism and rationalism, he offers readers a deeper understanding of love, leading to the relationship between love and hope. This is an encouraging and inspiring work."

Bishop Peter J. Elliott, Director, Associated Session, John Paul II Institute, Melbourne.

Fr Joel Wallace is a priest of the diocese of Wagga Wagga, Australia. He is currently studying for a doctorate in Sacred Theology at the Pontifical John Paul II Institute in Rome.

Learning to Love

at the School of John Paul II and Benedict XVI

Livio **Melina**

Translated by Joel Wallace

GRACEWING

Originally published in 2011
by Modotti Press,
an imprint of Connor Court Publishing Pty Ltd, Australia

This edition 2011

Gracewing
2 Southern Avenue
Leominster
Herefordshire HR6 0QF
www.gracewing.co.uk

ISBN 978 0 85244 778 9

Original cover design: Richard de Stoop

Contents

Preface

"Love is not something that is learned, and yet, there is nothing else as important to learn! *As a young priest, I learned to love human love*. This is one of the fundamental themes of my priesthood - my ministry in the pulpit, in the confessional and also in my writing. If one loves human love, there naturally arises the need to commit oneself completely to the service of *fair love*. Indeed, love is *beautiful*. After all, young people always seek the beauty in love; they want their love to be beautiful".[1]

With these words, found in his interview with the Italian journalist, Giovanni Messori, John Paul II unveils the inner secret of his extraordinary attention to human love, to marriage and to the family which he felt from the outset of his priesthood as an interior prompting of the Spirit and a true calling. Following this calling, he guided the Church, both as shepherd and teacher, with his extraordinary Wednesday Catecheses on human love in the divine plan, from September 5, 1979 to November 28, 1984,[2] with the establishment of the Pontifical Council for the Family in 1981 which promotes the pastoral care of the family and of human life in the universal Church, and the foundation of the Pontifical Institute for Studies of Marriage and Family which carries his name and guards the legacy, bearing the task of deepening, at the scientific level, the truth of human love, the person and the family and of

[1] John Paul II, *Crossing the threshold of hope*, Jonathon Cape, London, 1994, p. 123.
[2] Cf. John Paul II, *Uomo e donna lo creò. Catechesi sull'amore umano*, Città Nuova – Libreria Editrice Vaticana, Rome 1985. See also the edition: John Paul II, *L'amore umano nel piano divino: la redenzione del corpo e la sacramentalità del matrimonio nelle catechesi del mercoledì (1979-1984)*, Gilfredo Marengo (Ed.), Libreria Editrice Vaticana (Pontificio Istituto Giovanni Paolo II Per Studi su Matrimonio e Famiglia) 2009.

forming laity and priests at the academic and pastoral level.

The Russian theologian, Pavel Evdokimov, observed: "No one among the poets and thinkers has found the answer to the question: What is love?... Do you want to imprison the light? It will escape through your fingers"[3] It is precisely for this reason that he speaks of the need to return to the idea of "mystery" which, far from indicating what is unknown and unknowable, instead points to the way in which something is revealed and communicated insofar as it surpasses our cognitive and expressive capacity.

Nothing is as important to know and to encounter as love. In his first encyclical as Pope, Wojtyła expressed the same thought: "Man cannot live without love. He remains for himself an incomprehensible being, his life remains without meaning if love is not revealed to him, if he does not encounter love, if he does not experience it, if he does not make it his own, if he does not participate intimately in it".[4]

His successor, Benedict XVI, who also confessed himself to be his devoted disciple and spiritual son,[5] has echoed his work, dedicating the inaugural encyclical of his pontificate to the very centre of the Christian life: "God is Love": "So we know and believe the love God has for us" (*1 Jn* 4:16). Indeed, "Being Christian is not the result of an ethical choice or a lofty idea, but the encounter with an event, a person, which gives life a new horizon and a decisive direction".[6]

Love can be known only by means of that unique combination, involving not just reason but the person as such in a gratuitous experience that calls for freedom and involves the affections, calling him to a response of his whole life. We do not come to know love through chemical analysis of what happens in our

---

[3] P. Evdokimov, *Il sacramento dell'amore*, Milano 1983, p. 121.

[4] John Paul II, *Redemptor hominis*, n. 10.

[5] J. Ratzinger - Benedetto XVI, *Giovanni Paolo II. Il mio amato predecessore*, San Paolo, Cinisello Balsamo, 2007.

[6] Benedict XVI, *Deus caritas est*, n. 1.

brain when we love. We do not come to know it through logical analysis of the concepts that we use or through introspection with its subjective and sentimental emphasis. Rather, we come to know love in the unity of personally lived experience attested to by the great witnesses of love, particularly by the greatest Witness to love, who is Jesus. "By this we know love, that he laid down his life for us" (*1 Jn* 3:16). In action, specifically in the action of giving his life, he has shown us what love truly is.

Love can be known only when it is revealed. When it is revealed, it enlightens man as to the meaning of his life. It is manifested in beauty and in truth. Interest in human love implies a concern that it be "beautiful". Therefore, it involves a patient search for what is "true" and for what is "good". This truth is inscribed into the very heart of the person as an intimate call to the gift of self, fully revealed in Christ who alone reveals man to himself and makes known to him the sublimity of his vocation.[7]

Moreover, it is one thing to experience love and another to truly learn to love. *Love* is something which happens, which enthralls by what it promises; it changes life by opening up new perspectives. *To love* is a free action of the person who, by responding to the event of love, constructs a human history, which is lived out in a relationship with the other, taking account of the time and circumstances of life. In other words, we cannot content ourselves with experiencing the intensity of affection; it is necessary to nurture the relationship to which affectivity invites and to make it a commitment which bears fruit in individual and in social life.[8]

Let us take up again the question expressed in the title of this volume: how can we *teach others to love*? The crucial question of pastoral commitment to the young comes into conflict with a paradox which John Paul II did not directly respond to in his

---

[7] Cf. Vatican II, *Gaudium et spes,* n. 22.

[8] In this regard, see: F. Botturi – C. Vigna (Editors), *Affetti e legami*, "Annuario di etica" 1/2004, Vita e pensiero, Milano 2004.

interview with Messori. Why? Perhaps we can advance a hypothesis: by the very nature of the "mystery" of love, the answer cannot be given in words, that is, with a theory. It must be proposed, instead, as a personal journey to be undertaken by the witness of a life grounded in love and made beautiful by the truth. Only a saint can authentically teach us to love.

In order to learn to love, I propose in this volume that we listen to two great contemporary teachers – John Paul II and Benedict XVI: two popes, so distinct from each other in terms of their temperament, personal history and formation, yet so extraordinarily related and of one heart in testifying to the primacy of love and to its human and Christian truth.

John Paul II, in his personal, philosophical reflections as much as in his pontifical Magisterium, underlined the anthropological grandeur of love. Between the question of love and the question of man, a perichoresis exists, a vital circularity: love reveals the person who discovers the truth of himself only when he loves. This is precisely because "love is the name of the person", the point in which the unrepeatable uniqueness of every human being is manifested and fulfilled, who is willed by God himself and called to achieve his fullness by means of a sincere gift of self, apart from which, his life is bankrupt.[9]

Benedict XVI, continuing this line of thought, has illustrated the reciprocal implications that exist between the question of God and the question of love. He follows a pointer of St Augustine, according to which access to the inner mystery of God, one and triune, is achieved by the Christian's life of charity. In this way, authentic love acquires the value of a testimony, especially in a world suffering a dramatic atrophy of the religious sense.

Human acting, which gives hospitality to the Holy Spirit, can be a unique testimony to the glory of God, a true epiphany among men. In particular, Christian marriage and family acquire

---

[9] *Gaudium et spes*, n. 24.

a permanent sacramental significance for the world: precisely by achieving an authentic communion of persons in charity, they are called to witness to the salvific presence of God among men, which renders love possible.

The divine image in man is actuated when human beings express the communion of persons, showing themselves capable of the fruitful gift of themselves. The human body, which carries in itself the sign of sexual difference, implies a specific orientation to spousal love. This orientation is both dynamic and dramatic. It is a way toward an encounter in which freedom is called into play.

The *analogy* of love implies likeness within an always greater unlikeness: human love can be realized only by recognizing the absolute priority of a created love which precedes it and is offered to it as a light and strength so as to actuate it according to truth. At the same time, it is the *category* of the revelation of Trinitarian love which reveals to man the ultimate meaning of his human love, in the symbolism of the love of Christ, the Bridegroom, for the Church, his Spouse.

This then is the scope of the present text. It gathers together, in slightly revised and harmonized form, some interventions and studies, developed on various occasions and in different circumstances but linked together by a common thread of inspiration and a conceptual progression so that the presentations can be read as an organic unity in a single volume.

The first chapter, "Love in the horizon of responsibility", illustrates the thought of Karol Wojtyła, beginning with the question of how love and responsibility, together with the emotional and affective dimensions, can be united in freedom. It deals with a decisive question, on which the very possibility of ethics depends. An adequate response requires that the concepts of love and moral responsibility must be examined deeply in the light of experience and reason and on the basis of an authentic personalism.

The second chapter, "The nuptial body and its vocation to love" is dedicated to a re-reading of the theology of the body, which John Paul II developed in the great Wednesday Catecheses concerning human love in the divine plan. In confronting the problematic of contemporary culture in relation to intimacy, it becomes clear how decisive and precious is the contribution of the "theology of the body" for grasping the meaning of the sexual difference as a vocation to love and the resulting nexus between the language of the body and acts of sexual love.

The third chapter, "Man-woman: the archetype of love", taking the lead from a crucial statement of Pope Benedict XVI in his encyclical *Deus caritas est,* illustrates the elementary grammar of love. It is established on the sexual difference between man and woman, on the call to a communion of persons in *one flesh* and on fruitful openness to the transmission of life, all constitutive elements of the nuptial mystery.[10]

The fourth chapter, "The analogy of spousal love", traces the journey of theological maturation, witnessed to in magisterial teachings, from the encyclical of Paul VI, *Humanae vitae*, to *Deus caritas est* of Pope Benedict XVI, passing through *Familiaris consortio* and the Catecheses concerning *human love in the divine plan* of John Paul II. On the question of conjugal sexuality, it is not simply the problem of casuistry at stake, but the truth itself of man and woman, called to express their specific likeness to God who is love in an integrally human love, lived as a gift of self and open to the communication of the gift of life.

The fifth and final chapter is dedicated to "The gift that allows us to hope". By means of a somewhat provocative comparison between *Spe salvi* and *Gaudium et spes,* the ultimate horizon of hope is opened, allowing us to love: generated by love, hope opens a future to love and in this way sustains the tension of freedom in

[10] The expression qualifies the understanding of love developed in the theological anthropology of A. Scola, *Il mistero nuziale. 1. Uomo-Donna*, Pul-Mursia, Roma 1998; *2. Matrimonio-Famiglia*, Pul-Mursia, Roma 2000.

the arduous circumstances of life.[11]

In making this slim volume available to the public, my wish is that it may contribute to deepening appreciation for that "theology of love" delineated in the fundamental treatments of John Paul II and Benedict XVI. The Church has need of this that she may manifest the fascinating beauty of life according to the Gospel. In our day, man thirsts for this as he seeks to escape both from the aridity of moralism and the false illusions of permissivism.

Faced with Nietzsche's still widespread suspicion, according to which Christianity has poisoned eros and embittered life's most beautiful thing, it is hoped that this book will be a small contribution to welcoming the enthralling invitation made by Pope Benedict in the inaugural discourse of his pontificate, echoing the words of his beloved predecessor: "If we let Christ into our lives, we lose nothing, nothing, absolutely nothing of what makes life free, beautiful and great… Do not be afraid of Christ! He takes nothing away, and he gives you everything. When we give ourselves to him, we receive a hundredfold in return. Yes, open, open wide the doors to Christ – and you will find true life".[12]

Livio Melina
6th January, 2009, Epiphany of the Lord

Allow me briefly to offer a word of thanks to Dr Maria Chiara Di Pasquale, who, with intelligence and generous availability, helped me to fine-tune the text and to Fr Joel Wallace for the competent work of translation into English. Thank you also to Dr Colin Patterson for his revision of the translation.

[11] Cf. J. Noriega, "Cuando el amor se trasforma en esperanza", in J. Granados – J. Noriega (eds.), *La esperanza ancla y estrella. En torno a la encíclica* Spe Salvi, ed. Monte Carmelo, Burgos 2008, 127-143.
[12] Benedict XVI, *Homily at Mass for the inauguration of the pontificate of Pope Benedict XVI*, April 24, 2005.

1
Love in the Horizon of Responsibility according to Karol Wojtyła

Love, love pulsating the temples,
Love in man becomes thought and will:
Teresa's will to be in Andrew; Andrew's will to be in Teresa.
'Tis strange yet necessary to distance a little from the other,
Since man cannot remain in the other without end,
And he suffices not.
How can you achieve this, Teresa? How can you remain in Andrew forever?
How can you achieve this, Andrew? How can you remain in Teresa forever?
How can it be done if one cannot endure in the other? If man suffices not?[13]

These are the words of the chorus at the end of the first act of Karol Wojtyła's *The Jeweller's Shop*. They were written in 1960, at the same time as his work, *Love and Responsibility*, to accompany his developing philosophical reflection in the poetic language of drama and through lived experience. Love is not merely one adventure among others; far more than that, love is a task or a challenge that involves the whole person and determines his destiny. How can love endure forever? How can it achieve the communion of persons promised in the fascination of the first encounter? Above all, how much of this task of love depends on human freedom? These are the questions of the drama which underlie the philosophical approach of Wojtyła's *Love and Responsibility*.

[13] K. Wojtyła, *The Jeweller's Shop: A meditation on the Sacrament of Matrimony, passing on occasion into a drama*, Ignatius Press, San Francisco, 1980, p. 41.

1. Love in the horizon of responsibility

Love and responsibility: the association of these two terms in the volume's title can almost sound contradictory to our sensibility and might frighten us away from looking deeper at the schema that makes their association possible. The object of the work is to "give reasons for the norms of Catholic sexual ethics" by reference to the "more fundamental goods and values", among which the good of the person must be emphasized.[14] Accordingly, it is "love which constitutes the characteristic good of the world of persons". The specific theme of Wojtyła's essay is to "put love into love", that is, to introduce love, understood as everything that originates from the sexual impulse between man and woman, to love's horizon, understood as the ethical responsibility of one person toward the other.

To reach this objective, the first thing to be done is to overcome the reductive interpretations of the sexual experience and of love which would prevent us integrating love and personal responsibility. In Wojtyła's work, we can find reference to three main reductions which foil an adequate understanding of the experience of love.

Firstly, the naturalistic interpretation which, starting from the scientific objectification of the biological and physiological dynamisms of the body, reduces sexuality to libido and therefore to the mechanical world of nature, undermining in this way the sphere of ethics.[15] According to this interpretation, sexuality belongs to a sub-personal dimension which necessarily dominates all of nature's aspects. In this perspective, man himself is distinct from the passive functions of his body and if, on the one hand, he is completely determined at the level of his instincts, on the other hand, he emerges as spirit, claiming to be able to manipulate the body according to the exercise of his autonomous freedom.[16]

---

[14] K. Wojtyła, *Love and Responsibility*, Ignatius, San Francisco, 1981, p. 16.

[15] Ibid., pp. 61-63.

[16] The extreme fruit of this reductionism is the current "gender theory". See, for example: J. Butler, *Gender Trouble: Feminism and the Subversion of Identity*, Routledge, London 1990: For a critique: P. Donati, "La famiglia come relazione di «gender»", in Idem., *Manuale di sociologia della famiglia*, Laterza, Bari 1999, pp. 123-180.

The seemingly opposed romantic interpretation of love[17] emphasizes love as *passion*, considering this to be the essence of love: an irrational event which avoids any possibility of control on the part of freedom or of principles. The sexual dimension is subordinated to sentiment: the body remains absorbed in the turbulence of passion. The measure of love becomes the intensity of the feelings which are experienced. One rejoices aesthetically in the affective experience of the moment but without opening to the reality of a relationship with the other or to the building up, in time, and publically, of a shared life together.

However, Wojtyła also considers the scholastic interpretation of love which prevails in Catholic thought to be insufficient. This interpretation is characterized by an "anthropology of the faculties" which divides the human act into many partial acts attributed separately to the faculties of reason and will[18] and defined by their partial objects without reference to personal subjectivity. This theoretical model, proposing an extrinsic control of reason over the dynamisms of instinct and affectivity, is unable to grasp the dynamic unity of love and neglects its interpersonal context.

Underlying these reductive interpretations of human love which remain dialectically opposed and contrasting is a common deficiency: they all fail to adequately consider the person as the subject of love, in his relationship with the other person. For Wojtyła, the solution does not involve the superimposition of a new theory, more comprehensive than these last, but, above all, a re-encounter with the original experience of love so as to adequately consider all of its constitutive factors.

In this study, he applies for the first time a method perfected in his *Lubliner Vorlesungen* (1954-1957).[19] It concerns an original integration of the phenomenology taken above all from the school of Max

[17] Op., cit., *Love and Responsibility*, p. 109-113.

[18] In this regard: G. Angelini, *Eros e agape. Oltre l'alternativa*, Glossa, Milano 2006, pp. 23ff, 32ff, 63ff.

[19] K. Wojtyła, *Lubliner Vorlesungen*, Seewald Verlag, Stuttgart 1981 For an excellent approach to this work: K.L. Schmitz, *At the Center of the Human Drama. The Philosophical Anthropology of Karol Wojtyła / Pope John Paul II*, CUA Press, Washington DC 1993, pp. 30-57.

Scheler, but critically evaluated in its constitutive limits by enlisting the perspective of the ontological realism of St Thomas Aquinas.[20] The first step consists in grasping the essential elements of phenomena and the important relationships among them; the second step consists in illumining the essence of the phenomenon, situating it in the context of the human person in his totality and his interpersonal relationships.[21] In this way, the perspective of the subject proper to modernity is assumed without falling into subjectivism precisely because "every subject is at the same time an objective being; he is objectively something or someone", as Wojtyła says at the beginning of the text.[22] At the same time, it is the perspective of the person, not just of the substance, which constitutes the culmination of metaphysics and, therefore, impinges upon ontology, especially the interpretation of love.

However, beyond the philosophical references, the author's ultimate point of reference is lived experience: the book "does not constitute the exposition of a doctrine; rather, it represents before all else the fruit of a constant engagement between doctrine and life", developed in the daily exercise of pastoral activity.[23] So we have here the meaning of the method adopted by Wojtyła: reference to experience is not exhausted in the analysis of content in order to grasp its significance, but in receptivity to its reality as something greater than ourselves.[24]

True, it is an experience of love; but it is also an experience of responsibility. Surprising as it may seem, we must observe that this concept is quite a recent one in ethical reflection, given that it was introduced only in the first decades of the 20th Century by Max

[20] Concerning the method of this work, see: R. Buttiglione, *Il pensiero di Karol Wojtyła,* Jaca Book, Milano 1982, pp. 103-114; J. Kupczak, *Destined for Liberty. The Human Person in the Philosophy of Karol Wojtyła/Pope John Paul II*, CUA Press, Washington DC 2000, pp. 63-81.

[21] Wojtyła does not clearly separate these two moments in *Love and Responsibility,* although it is more noticeable in the second part. It will be more noticeable in the theoretical work, *Person and Act* of 1969, K. Wojtyła, *The Acting Person,* Reidel, Dordrecht, Holland, 1979, pp. 3-22 where he introduces his methodology.

[22] Op. cit., *Love and Responsibility,* p. 24.

[23] Ibid., p. 15.

[24] Cf. J.J. Pérez-Soba, *La experiencia moral,* Facultad de Teología 'San Dámaso', Madrid 2002.

Weber.[25] To introduce it critically, we must clarify three variables that are implicit: that which is relative to the subject of responsibility (*who* is responsible?); that which refers to the object which he is responsible for (*what* is he responsible for?); and, lastly, the variable of intersubjectivity (*before whom* is he responsible?). The analysis of responsibility points us toward the context of the experience of moral praxis and, specifically, toward the connection between person and act. We see in *Love and Responsibility* that Wojtyła always conducts his analysis of love parallel to his analysis of moral experience. This is particularly significant: for him, love is not just a gratifying event which occurs at the level of the emotions, but an invitation to love, that is, to learn a way in which freedom achieves the promise of fulfilling what is given seminally in the experience of love.

2. The experience of love and the revelation of the person

The adoption of experience as the point of departure for the analysis of love implies for Wojtyła the consideration of some of its constitutive elements. We shall demonstrate at least three such fundamental aspects. Firstly, there is the personal and interpersonal context in which such experience occurs: beyond the multiplicity and complexity of its factors, "love is always a reciprocal relationship of persons", an event of the person and an event among persons.[26]

[25] This work in based on: *Amor y responsabilidad y en el ensayo fenomenológico del maestro de* K. Wojtyła: R. Ingarden, *Sulla responsabilità*, Italian translation by A. Setola, Cseo, Bologna, 1982. The classic points of reference for ethics are: M. Weber, *Politik als Beruf* (1919) (Italian translation.: *La scienza come professione. La politica come professione*, Einaudi, Torino 2004); H. Richard Niebuhr, *The responsible Self. An Essay in Christian Moral Philosophy*, Westminster John Knox Press, Louisville Kentucky 1999 (1st edition: 1963); H. Jonas, *Il principio responsabilità. Un'etica per la civiltà tecnologica*, Einaudi, Torino 1993 (German original: 1979); P. Ricoeur, *Il concetto di responsabilità*, in Idem., Il Giusto, SEI, Torino 1998, pp. 31-56; P. Ricoeur, *Sé come un altro*, Jaca Book, Milano 1993 (French original: 1990). For a general presentation: A. Fumagalli, "Interpersonalità, comunità e responsabilità", in L. Melina – D. Granada (Editors), *Limiti alla responsabilità? Amore e giustizia*, Lup, Roma 2005, pp. 119-134.

[26] Op. cit., *Love and Responsibility*, pp. 67-68.

This is the concrete point of departure that enables us to avoid the abstraction and objectification of the phenomenon of love, which tends, fatally, to identify love with only one of its partial components. It is precisely in reference to the person that all other factors must be assumed: the impulses of the body and the psychological dynamics of affectivity and of feelings.

Moving on to the second element, the body is always considered as a living body which reflects a personal interiority and intentionality directed toward the reality of the exterior world. Certainly, the analysis of the human sciences, particularly that of physiology, finds its place here and it is considered very carefully in *Love and Responsibility.* However, the author is always careful to avoid allowing the reductive factors which influence the method of these sciences to prevail over the concrete experience of love.

Finally, the experience of love always implies personal freedom, which is expressed in action. The practical mediation of acting is the concrete place where love is realized. In this way, Wojtyła makes room, right at the beginning of the volume, for an analysis of the verbs "to use" and "to enjoy", as an expression of those actions in which the person is at the same time both the "subject and object of action".

In the experience of love, the profound connection between love and person emerges, which constitutes that central nucleus of Wojtyła's reflection and brings him closer to the philosophical current of French personalism of the last century.[27] Referring to the Holy Spirit, St Thomas Aquinas said, in the context of his Trinitarian theology, "Love is the name of the person".[28] The statement has an anthropological extension: only the person is worthy of love and only love enables an authentic relationship between persons. It is

[27] It is sufficient to mention, among others: J. Lacroix, *Personne et amour*, Seuil, Paris 1955 and M. Nédoncelle, *Vers une philosophie de la personne et de l'amour*, Aubier-Montaigne, Paris 1957. For a complete panoramic view and a critical approach: J.-J. Pérez-Soba, *La pregunta por la persona. La respuesta de la interpersonalidad. Estudio de una categoría personalista*, Facultad de Teología 'San Dámaso', Madrid 2004.

[28] St Thomas Aquinas, *Summa Theologiae*, I, q. 37, a. 1. On this subject, see: J.-J. Pérez-Soba, *"Amor es nombre de persona". Estudio de la interpersonalidad en el amor en Santo Tomás de Aquino*, Pul- Mursia, Roma 2001.

impossible to understand love except in the perspective of the person; on the other hand, it is impossible to understand the person except in the light of love. So what is it that manifests the personal experience of love? What do we gain from assuming the personalistic perspective when considering love?

In the first place, it is love that reveals the person. Philosophical reflection affirms that man is "someone" and this distinguishes him from other beings of the visible world that are always and only "something". He is a subject and can never be considered merely as an object. The term person was chosen to underline that man is not enclosed in the notion of an "individual of a species", as Wojtyła points out. In him, there is something more, namely, a fullness and perfection of particular being which cannot be expressed in any other way than with the word "person".[29] However, it is precisely love which leads us to understand that the person in his singularity is irreducible to any other category of thought.[30] In love, the beloved is unique and unrepeatable; she is revealed to be non-substitutable by any other. In fact, love has for its object, not the common qualities of the species, nor the singular qualities of the individual as such, which could very well be found in others and perhaps in greater measure. On the contrary, its object is the person of the other in his singularity and mystery, in the destiny of fullness to which he is called and to which both feel attracted. On the other hand, only when love is developed to the point of touching the person at this level, then and only then, is it forever.

On the other hand, the person is open to a relationship with other persons, as one subject to another. Personhood is not individuality enclosed in self-sufficiency; it is freedom open to encounter and acceptance in which a person can find himself again as subject. It is precisely intersubjectivity, the recognition of the other in his

[29] K. Wojtyła, *Love and Responsibility*, cit., p. 24. Cf. R. Spaemann, *Personen. Versuche über den Unterschied zwischen "etwas" un "jemand"*, Klett-Cotta, Stuttgart 1996.

[30] A. Wierzbicki, *La persona e la morale. Introduzione*, in K. Wojtyła, *Metafisica della persona. Tutte le opere filosofiche e saggi integrativi* (edited by G. Reale and T. Styczen), Bompiani, Milano 2003, pp. 1219-1227. See in this regard: J. Crosby, *The Selfhood of the Human Person*, CUA Press, Washington DC 1996, pp. 41-81.

quality of subject, which prevents the person from being reduced to a mere object to "be used". However, Wojtyła wishes to emphasize something more: the communication which love consists in cannot remain merely within intersubjectivity because the person is not reducible to his consciousness. Interpersonality must involve the person in his integrity and therefore in his corporeity and be realized in a communication of the good.[31] Love is directed toward achieving a communion of persons based on a common orientation toward the good loved by both which, in this way, becomes the common good and establishes the relationship.

Secondly, only in love does the person achieve the fashioning of himself. Let us all take to heart the prophetic strength of the words of John Paul II in his first encyclical: "Man cannot live without love. He remains for himself an incomprehensible being, his life remains without meaning if love is not revealed to him, if he does not encounter love, if he does not experience it, if he does not make it his own, if he does not participate intimately in it".[32] Love, particularly sexual love, has a unique, existential value for the person: it decides the meaning or the meaninglessness of his life.

The call to freedom, that is, the reference to moral experience, is inserted precisely here. In effect, the person realizes himself as a person through his acts. The moral dimension of experience is constituted precisely by the inescapable bond that unites the person to his action on the strength of a call to the good which seeks to be achieved in a free response which decides the identity and meaning of the life of the one who acts.

At this point, the category of responsibility appears which enables us to relate moral experience to the experience of love: through my acting, I am called to respond to a presence filled with promise, which is given to me in an encounter. In this encounter, the gaze of the other is intentionally directed toward me. It precedes my action and opens it to meaning, precisely because it orientates it toward

---

[31] Op. cit., *Love and Responsibility*, pp. 73-79.

[32] John Paul II, *Redemptor hominis*, n. 10.

a good to be achieved, namely: the communion of persons.[33] The experience of love clarifies the meaning of the moral experience and of responsibility. The person is awakened to his moral subjectivity by the presence of the other person who calls him to respond to this primary and gratuitous gift of the loving presence, achieving in this way a communion in the good. We are accountable then for our acts, not for consequences that are exterior to them. Consideration of the experience of responsibility is necessary for overcoming the sphere of pure consciousness and of the pure "I" so as to embrace the person with all his characteristics.[34] Rightly therefore, Wojtyła's critique of utilitarianism is very severe since it denies personal responsibility in acting and represents a reduction of the truth of love.

The inadequacy of the question in which the Anglo-Saxon normative ethic has been swamped is clear: "Why must I be moral?" This question is born of a separation of the act from the concrete experience in which it becomes an act of the person. If morality is understood as a series of previously existing principles to be applied to action, then the question is understandable, but cannot be answered. However, in reality, morality is a constitutive dimension of experience and by asking itself the question, "Why must I be moral?" it is already, from the start, adopting an immoral posture toward life by undermining the responsibility that the experience of the other and the call to love inevitably imply.[35]

3. The dynamism of love

The experience of love, particularly the love between man and woman, has then a realistic and dynamic character. It is awakened by the

[33] Lévinas' reading is particularly important here, although the gaze of the other, for him, is resolved in the commandment and is not understood to be the presence of an original gift which invites one to follow a way and makes this way possible: E. Lévinas, *Totalité et Infini. Essai sur l'exteriorité*, Nijhoff, La Haye 1961, 230.

[34] For a critique of the limitations of Husserl and a clarification of the ontic fundamentals of responsibility, see R. Ingarden, *Sulla responsabilità*, op. cit. 69-76.

[35] Concerning this: J.J. Pérez-Soba, *La experiencia moral*, op. cit., p. 14.

concrete reality of a presence and is intentionally guided toward the other person so as to construct a communion with her. In the second part of *Love and Responsibility,* Wojtyła makes a careful analysis of the dynamism of love, distinguishing three dimensions: the psychological, the metaphysical and the moral. It is of interest to us here to detain ourselves above all with the first, integrating into it some elements of the second. We will dedicate the last part of the reflection, which will concern Karol Wojtyła's personalism, to the moral dimension.

Our first observation is that the author's analysis integrates the contribution of psychology and modern phenomenology. These point to the motivations which drive action. At the same time, he introduces a Thomistic analysis of the passions and the will, which enables us to discover the role of the end, that is, the ethical value for the personal will.[36] The individual elements of the analysis of the dynamism of love are not understood as isolated fragments but as integral parts of a single personal act of love. Partial aspects can only be understood in the unity of this act. Only from this united perspective do they receive their full intelligibility.

At the beginning of love, we find an experience of attraction. It begins by perception, that is, by the reaction of the senses and the excitement caused by their objects. Such a reaction is always accompanied by emotion, that is, by the psychological reaction not only to sexual values but also spiritual values which the encounter with the person brings. Sensuality, the complex sphere of response to masculinity or femininity through the body of the person of the opposite sex, is always linked to the recognition of personal values. Indeed, the body is an integral aspect of the person and can never be dissociated from him. If the corporal dimension is separated from the interpersonal context of the relationship, it will come to be characterized by a utilitarian and inevitably unstable orientation. Here we can locate the phenomenon of disordered desire which Catholic doctrine calls concupiscence and which implies an intentional reduction of the other to a mere object of pleasure. In this way, the body of the other is used without recognizing his or her personal value.

---

[36] Op. cit., *Love and Responsibility,* note 64.

However, a special experience of the value of the person as such is anticipated in the emotions. This experience concerns the deepest and most intense emotions related to the encounter with another human subject and to the promise of communion revealed in it.[37] In this sense, affectivity plays a decisive role. Wojtyła defines affectivity as the capacity to react to the person's masculinity or femininity with an appreciation for the person's complexity and not merely on account of sexual values considered in a narrow sense. The affective reaction is expressed in the "desire to always be together".[38]

Affection has a decisive importance in the dynamism of love because it leads to discovering the values of the other in a concrete way. Affective experience points essentially to the other as a person. In this sense, affectivity prepares reason and will respectively to understand and accept the person in his truth, beyond his usefulness and capacity to provide pleasure. It enables, even from the beginning, the unification of the various elements which interiorly drive one person toward another, on the basis of the recognition of a primary, gratifying gift, namely: the satisfaction experienced on account of the presence of the beloved, with an awareness that this corresponds to a profound longing of the heart. However, affectivity in itself remains ambiguous. For example, I can affectively withdraw into myself and take pleasure merely in what the other awakens in me, without going beyond myself and grasping the value of the other as a person.

Here is the true and proper level of love: to grasp, as a personal act and by a judgement of reason, the value of the person in and for himself and, by an act of the will, to seek what is truly good for him. There is a transcendent movement here in the dynamism of love which prevails over the concupiscible self-referencing of instinct or affectivity; by following the original orientation, the other is understood as a value in himself that merits his being recognized and affirmed for his own sake, in an act of ecstasy and dedication. The attraction of the sexual tendency and the experience of sympathy for the other, so characteristic of the affective moment, must be transformed into

[37] Ibid., pp. 74-80.

[38] Ibid., pp. 89-90.

friendship, the specific trait of which is benevolence, namely: to want the good of the other.

This is the characteristic formula of love. Here Wojtyła makes his own the affirmation of St Thomas, with all the richness of his interior analysis: *"In hoc precipue consistit amor, quod amans amato bonum velit" ("Love principally consists in this: that the lover wants the good for the beloved").*[39] Love is in the will as "the final authority; without its participation, no experience has full personal value or the gravity appropriate to the experiences of the human person".[40] The will's volition does not arise from a vacuum, as we have seen, but is formed by assuming the dynamisms of the sexual and affective tendencies. For its accomplishment, this act of the will must be founded on a rational judgement which grasps the unique and irreducible value of the person as such. In the development of the interpersonal relationship of love, the content that makes communication possible also appears, namely: the good whose truth establishes and determines the act of love.

So we come to what constitutes, simultaneously, love's essence and its paradox, that is, donation. "To give oneself" is more than just "to want". It implies a supreme act of freedom, which is found in a specific way in spousal love.[41] Now, how can a person who is by nature self-possessed, inalienable and non-substitutable (*sui juris et alteri incommunicabilis*) give himself to another in a true gift of self without thereby alienating himself? Personal maturity consists, for Wojtyła, in self-possession and self-mastery, by means of which the tendencies of the impulses and affections are ordered by the judgement of reason and facilitate the free self-determination of the personal subject.

At the same time, love constitutes the greatest realization of the person's intrinsic potentialities. Love culminates in going out of oneself in a free gift of self to the other person. It involves a paradox because "enrichment and personal growth" can only happen by means

[39] St Thomas Aquinas, *Contra gentiles*, III, c. 90 (Marietti n. 2657). This definition taken from Aristotle, *Rhetoric*, II, c. 4: 1380 b, 35-36.

[40] Op. cit., *Love and Responsibility*, p. 117.

[41] Ibid., pp. 99, 84, 117.

of this gift. Here is the secret of human freedom, which is born of a love and is made for love: the person, who belongs essentially to himself, can belong to the other only through a free act of his love. In the freedom of love, the person continues to possess himself but, simultaneously, is given totally to the other.

Of course, perceiving the echo, in advance, of the great anthropological affirmation of *Gaudium et spes,* John Paul II often loved to repeat: "…man, who is the only creature on earth which God willed for itself, cannot fully find himself except through a sincere gift of himself".[42] In this conciliar text, the two pillars of Wojtylian personalism present in *Love and Responsibility* come together, namely: the person as end; and the gift of self. The first pillar has its ultimate foundation in Christian theological anthropocentrism, admirably expressed by St Thomas Aquinas: "The ultimate end of the universe is God who only the intellectual creature attains by knowing and loving Him as He is in Himself. Therefore, in the whole universe, only the intellectual creature is desired for his own sake, so that all other realities exist in relationship to him.[43] The second pillar reaches back to the mysticism of St John of the Cross as has been convincingly documented.[44] The Spanish mystic spoke eloquently of the soul's "gift of self" to God, which is rooted in God's prior gift to the soul. It has a nuptial character and has its deepest root in Trinitarian love.[45]

---

[42] Vatican II, Pastoral Constitution, *Gaudium et spes*, n. 24. Concerning the concept of "donation" in Karol Wojtyła, see: G. Reale, *Karol Wojtyła, un pellegrino dell'assoluto*, Bompiani, Milano 2005, pp. 103-107; also: P. Ide, "Une théologie du don. Les occurrences de *Gaudium et spes*, n. 24, § 3 chez Jean-Paul II", in *Anthropotes* XVII/1 (2001), 149-178 (the first part of the article) and *Anthropotes* XVII/2 (2001), 313-344 (the second part).

[43] St Thomas Aquinas, *Summa contra gentiles*, III, c. 111 (Marietti, n. 2858): "Constat autem ex praemissis (cap. XVII) finem ultimum universi Deum esse, quem sola intellectualis natura consequitur in seipso, eum scilicet cognoscendo et amando, ut ex dictis (Ch. XXV ff.) patet. Sola igitur intellectualis natura est propter se quaesita in universo, alia autem omnia propter ipsam"..

[44] Cf. M. Waldstein, *Introduction,* in John Paul II, *Man and Woman He Created Them. A Theology of the Body.* Translation, Introduction, and Index by Michael Waldstein, Pauline Books & Media, Boston 2006, pp. 23-34, where he speaks of "Wojtyła's Carmelite personalism".

[45] Cf. St John of the Cross, *Fiamma viva d'amore* B, 3, § 78-80, in *Opere*, 4th edition, Postulazione Generale dei Carmelitani Scalzi, Roma 1979, 818-820. (In English: *The Works of St John of the Cross,* Vol. 3, London, Burns, Oats & Washbourne, 1947, *The living flame of love,* pp. 15-226).

The originality of the moral perspective, when it speaks of the gift of self, consists in seeing it in its tension toward a good life, that is, in relationship to excellent acting which implies a life well-governed. Free acting, precisely insofar as it is directed to another person and to the gift of self, calls the person to a communion and enables him not only to "subsist in himself" but also "to subsist in communion", experienced in the act of love.[46]

If the essence of love is donation, we can understand why, according to the author of *Love and Responsibility,* the love of a man and a woman in the context of marriage, which is certainly only one particular context of love, represents the place where the totality of love's characteristics is reflected with particular clarity. We cannot disregard the profound agreement here with the central statements of the first encyclical of Pope Benedict XVI, *Deus caritas est:* "Amid this multiplicity of meanings, however, one in particular stands out: love between man and woman, where body and soul are inseparably joined and human beings glimpse an apparently irresistible promise of happiness. This would seem to be the very epitome of love; all other kinds of love immediately seem to fade in comparison".[47]

4. The truth of love

As we approach the end of this chapter, let us now return to a popular Wojtylian expression, already encountered, which is decisive for grasping the meaning of his personalism. I am referring to the expression, the "truth of love".[48] The moment of truth is highlighted as necessary in order to prevail over the ambiguities of the spontaneous

[46] Cf. J. Noriega, "La prospettiva morale del 'dono di sé'", in G. Grandis – J. Merecki (Editors), *L'esperienza sorgiva. Persona – Comunione – Società. Studi in onore del Prof. Stanisław Grygiel*, "Sentieri della verità" n. 2: Cattedra Wojtyła, Cantagalli, Siena 2007, pp. 53-60.

[47] Benedicto XVI, Encyclical Letter, *Deus caritas est*, n. 2. See in this respect: L. Melina - C. Anderson (ed.), *La vìa del amor. Reflexiones sobre la encìclica* Deus caritas est *de Benedicto XVI*, Monte Carmelo – Pontifical John Paul II Institute for Studies on Marriage and Family, Burgos 2006.

[48] See especially the following paragraphs: op. cit., *Love and Responsibility*, pp. 114-118; 135-137.

impulses and of affectivity so that the freedom of love may emerge, that is, the capacity to affirm the person for his own sake. However, a new difficulty seems to arise precisely here. According to the most wide-spread opinion, as Wojtyła explains, love is related above all to the subjective truth of sentiment,[49] to authenticity; it avoids truth imposed from the outside, which would be purely intellectual, disconnected from life and would impose its criteria and rules on experience extrinsically. The question is then: how can we overcome the subjectivism of a "love without truth", without falling into an intellectualism of a "truth without love"?

The road travelled in *Love and Responsibility* explores the logic proper to love from the inside. This road begins with the importance offered by the very experience of love which contains already the necessary reference to the good in any truly loving, interpersonal relationship. A love which wants the good for the beloved is authentic, that is, it is oriented toward a true and real good, in a way that conforms to the nature of that good.[50] It is not just that "I desire you as a good for me", but that "I desire your good", "I desire what is truly a good for you". This requires a certain level of disinterest so as to affirm the objectivity of truth in relation to the good; it is constituted neither for me nor for the other but refers to the objective reality of personal goods, as the Creator planned them.

On the other hand, every appreciation of the good is realized in a communicative environment, between persons and by means of a language which implies a certain objectivity based on the rational content of the good. Precisely in this way, the wills of those who love are found to be united in a new and particular bond, namely: the recognition of the "common good" which is truly good for each of them.[51]

We seem to have evidence here, within the dynamic of love, of reference to a truth concerning the good that has its ultimate origin in God the Creator. It is the very condition of possibility and

---

[49] Ibid., pp. 80-82.

[50] Ibid., p. 91.

[51] Ibid., p. 38.

authenticity for love itself in its effective "exodus" toward the other. Therefore, Wojtyła dedicates the fourth part of his work to the theme of justice toward the Creator, affirming in this way that there is an at least implicit and unavoidable reference to God in every experience of love. The argument of *Love and Responsibility* is always developed on a rigorously philosophical rather than theological plane, although it is always open to theology. The reference to God the Creator belongs to a truly rational reflection concerning human love. Such a reference provides the foundation that sustains and defines its nature, determining the norms that govern it: an original love precedes and establishes the human love which necessarily has an analogical and responsorial/dialogical character.

At the level of the contents proper to the good, on which conjugal love is based, the traditional doctrine of the Church had pointed to the objective content of marriage in terms of three ends: procreation, mutual help and the remedy for concupiscence. A personalistic perspective such as Wojtyła's remains unsatisfied with any attempt to establish the union of man and woman merely on these foundations. Only love is an adequate attitude of one person toward another. Some early forms of personalism applied to sexual morality had proposed a revision of the doctrine of the ends, identifying love *tout court* with mutual love and making this the primary finality of marriage. This reduced procreation to a secondary, merely biological end and eliminated the reference to concupiscence as an expression that might promote a now surpassed, negative vision of sexuality.[52] Instead, for Wojtyła, it would be profoundly reductive and an extrinsicism to consider love as just one of the ends of marriage. Love is the very substance of marriage. It regulates it from within and the traditional ends acquire their moral significance from it. On the other hand, it is not the biological finality as such that establishes the ethical value to be respected: that would be naturalism. Rather, precisely in the light of the experience of love, the moral significance of sexuality

[52] Obviously, we are referring, above all, to H. Doms, *Significato e scopo del matrimonio*, Cathedra, Roma 1946. For a critical reading: A. Mattheeuws, *Union et procréation. Développements de la doctrine des fins du mariage*, Cerf, Paris 1989; G. Mazzocato, 'Il dibattito tra Doms e neotomisti sull'indirizzo personalista', in *Teologia* 31 (2006), 249-275.

appears in relation to those goods, which belong to the nature of the person himself.[53] So there is no need to rearrange their hierarchy or find error in their meaning: the ends of marriage are the concrete determinations which the truth of love involves in the sexual sphere so that the goods to which they tend may be realized.[54]

The truth of love demands the attitude of respect which Wojtyła calls the personalistic norm, a fundamental point of his entire ethical thought which he takes up again and integrates starting from the well-known Kantian formulation: "Whenever a person is the object of your acting, remember that you must not treat him only as a means, as an instrument; rather, he is, or ought to be an end in himself".[55] The heart of the sexual moral problem consists then in this: How can one "enjoy sexual pleasure without treating the person as an object of pleasure"?[56] Sexual morality will consist then in an ongoing synthesis and an ever increasing maturity of the natural finalities of the sexual tendency and the personalistic norm. More precisely, it will consist in assuming, within the naturalistic perspective of love, those goods for the person which are constitutive of his nature.[57]

The truth concerning the good illumines the way of personal love from within and facilitates the ordering of the tendencies of instinct and affectivity. This is the decisive dimension of the moral virtues, by means of which the appetitive dynamisms are shaped and orientated toward the good of the person, becoming in this way a positive energy in favour of a fully human expression of sexual love. Through the virtues, particularly chastity, the acting subject achieves integration; the fragmentation and disintegration of concupiscence is overcome in this way and the personalistic norm is perceived to be connatural to the subject.[58] Affectivity plays a decisive role in this

[53] See in particular the importance of note 19 in op.cit., *Love and Responsibility*, p. 294.

[54] Cf. R. Buttiglione, *Il pensiero*, op.cit., pp. 120-121.

[55] Cf. Op.cit., *Love and Responsibility*, pp. 40-43.

[56] Ibid., p. 67.

[57] Cfr. L. Melina - J.-J. Pérez-Soba (Editors), *Il bene e la persona nell'agire*, Lup, Roma, 2002.

[58] The entire third part of *Love and responsibility* is dedicated to the topic of chastity. For a systematic development of a sexual morality in the perspective of the virtues, see: J. Noriega, *El destino del eros. Perspectivas de moral sexual*, Palabra, Madrid 2004.

transformation of the subject and in this interiorizing of the personal truth of love. Particularly involved are the great and profound emotions which, in the experience of love, accompany and precede the recognition of the unique value of the person loved. In this way, the truth concerning love, rather than being imposed from outside the subject, is recognized as intrinsic to his sensibility. It is the most intimate and secret substance which reason illuminates and guides to its fullness. The exercise of freedom, sustained by grace, contributes by impressing this truth on the affective orientations as the personal life of the individual increases in excellence. And this virtue is not extrinsic to the interpersonal context either, because it is clearly evident in the relationship between those who love.

Conclusion

How can that love which *pulsates the temples* last forever? How can that love which glimpsed the promise of communion in the fascination of the first encounter endure in the ongoing construction of a common destiny? The question of Andrew and Teresa in *The Jeweller's Shop* has been explored with diligence and depth in the reflections of *Love and Responsibility*. Having treated the question as decisively existential, since life's entire destiny depends on love, the search for increasingly adequate ways of response must now be embarked upon and continually be deepened.

At the end of this journey, we can say that the personalistic way, pointed out by Karol Wojtyła, is always relevant and promising in the convincing response that it offers the men and women of today. This is primarily because it presents the experience of love as that place where the unique and unrepeatable value of the person and his vocation to the gift of self is revealed. It is also because a concrete approach to the dynamic unity of the person and his acting enables us to re-establish a positive nexus between freedom and truth, overcoming in this way the unilateral oppositions of, on the one hand, subjectivism which reduces love to a subjective authenticity and, on the other hand, objectivism which misunderstands personalistic richness.

Only that love which becomes a responsible act of the person can endure in time.

2

The Nuptial Body and its Vocation to Love in the Catecheses of John Paul II

"I set out to write on sex. I found myself writing just as much about love; and about gender". With these words, the English sociologist, Anthony Giddens, introduces his important volume, *The Transformation of Intimacy* which testifies to the impossibility, also in our times, of speaking about sexuality outside of the context of love.[59] He shows that the contemporary shift in the way of understanding the sexually differentiated body, to which a total plasticity has been attributed, developed from the romantic idea of love. The claim is advanced today that sexuality and love can be considered apart from the body's natural determinations, even to the extent of dissolving the meaning of the masculine/feminine difference. This has occurred, not only at the private level, but also in the normative, public sphere of society. So the body increasingly assumes a political relevance and enters the milieu of sociological interests. As Giddens maintains: "the changes now affecting sexuality are indeed revolutionary, and in a very profound way".[60]

The scenario is disquieting because it is profoundly destabilizing. It needs to be understood in its cultural and anthropological dimensions. It challenges theological anthropology in particular to rethink its foundational categories, if it is true – as Benedict XVI affirmed in the encyclical *Deus caritas est* – that "Amid this multiplicity of meanings... one in particular stands out: love between man and woman, where body and soul are inseparably joined and human beings glimpse an apparently irresistible promise of happiness. This would seem to be the very epitome of love; all other kinds of love immediately seem to

[59] A. Giddens, *The Transformation of Intimacy: sexuality, love and eroticism in modern societies*, Stanford University Press, CA, USA, 1993, p. 1.
[60] Ibid., p. 3.

fade in comparison" (*DCE* 2). The centrality of the anthropological man/woman theme is amplified by its association, developed a little later in the encyclical, with the theological theme in the light of biblical revelation according to which monogamous marriage, with its properties of indissolubility and exclusivity, corresponds to monotheism and to the image of that God who has revealed himself in the history of love with his people (cf. *DCE* 11).

How can we reflect on the unattainable originality of the male/female difference without falling into naturalism? Such naturalism would refuse to pass through the mediation of the consciousness of the subject, would ignore the dramatic nature of freedom and time and would also ignore the inescapable cultural dimension in which the existence of man and woman is lived out. On the other hand, how can we reconcile the motions of subjective experience with the irrevocable demand of the Christian message to witness to a truth of love between man and woman, already offered in creation and definitively manifested in revelation?

The questions summarily highlighted here need to be rigorously developed in the face of experience and of the prevailing mentality and culture. They suggest a re-reading of Tradition and of Scripture in particular. Such a plan has indeed been undertaken by the Magisterium itself, thanks to the work of John Paul II in the great cycle of *Catecheses on human love in the divine plan*, given from September 5, 1979 to November 28, 1984.[61] He made the profound purpose of this catechesis clear, motivated as he was by the desire to delineate the foundations of a "theology of the body". In this way, he sought to make up for certain current deficiencies in a tradition of thought which had not been able to adequately evaluate the human body or

[61] Cf. John Paul II, *Uomo e donna lo creò. Catechesi sull'amore umano*, Città Nuova – Libreria Editrice Vaticana, Rome 1985. Outstanding for its critical rigor and its introduction is the recent English edition: *Man and Woman He Created Them. A Theology of the Body*. Translation, Introduction, and Index by Michael Waldstein, Pauline, Boston 2006.

even make sense of the richness of the biblical data.[62]

Therefore, it is opportune to attempt a re-reading of this important magisterial teaching,[63] which may test the value of its response to the most burning questions of today, gathering the suggestions which eventually arise from anthropological and moral reflection. John Paul's catecheses will be divided into three basic sections, which the main themes of this chapter will take up again: the nuptial character of the body in the male/female difference which it connotes; the resulting vocation to love which is signaled as the dynamic and dramatic element; finally, the nexus between the language of the body and the acts of sexual love. Before pursuing such a re-reading, which will only be of a general nature, I think it will be useful to begin with a comparison with the current problems in relation to the nexus between the sexually differentiated body and love, specifically in comparison with the analyses of Anthony Giddens. This will provide the leading thread of the reflection on the question concerning the meaning of intimacy.

1. An empty intimacy: the body and love in the ambit of the "pure relationship"

According to the English sociologist, society today, which he calls late modernity, is experiencing a radical transformation of the interior sphere of existence. Sexuality and the affections belong intrinsically to this characteristically human interiority. In earlier times, this aspect of the personal life was mainly confined in privacy and was respected in its traditional configurations by the state. Recently, however, through the contemporary influx of two factors which converge in the feminist

[62] He speaks of this in Catecheses XLIV, XLV and XLVI, in op. cit., *Uomo e donna lo creò*. (English - referred to from now on: Catecheses (TOB) 44-46, pp. 301-314, op. cit., *Man and Woman He Created Them. A Theology of the Body*. He refers here to Manichaeism which appeared "at the margin of Christian thought" and even "dared to enter the land of Christianity", offering a gravely reductive and unilaterally negative interpretation of corporeity and sexuality.

[63] For a reflection on the magisterial value, cf: G. Angelini, "Indole pastorale e oggetto morale del magistero", in *Teologia* 15 (1990), pp. 150-171.

movement, namely: the democratic principle of the individual's total autonomy; and the possibility of sexuality freed from reproduction – the social form of the "pure relationship" has manifested itself. This approach to intimacy is based on a sexual, sentimental and emotional parity[64] understood as an encounter between equal and autonomous individuals[65] who negotiate the form and timeframe of a relationship, which is then established on an agreement about the balance of giving and having: such a relationship is defined as "pure", precisely because it cuts itself off from every form previously derived from nature or culture.

The democratic claim of each individual's autonomy underlies the purpose of every institutionalized dependency and demands a constant renegotiation of the relationship between the partners, each of whom will appreciate the other as long as his own interests are respected.[66] The "pure" relationship, distinguished from marriage, is only sustained on the basis of a "confluent" calculation of benefits, at the level of sentimental and sexual satisfaction, that each gains from continuing the relationship.

This transformation of interiority implies the idea of a "plastic sexuality", made possible by the complete separation of sex from the reproductive requirement.[67] The body now assumes a total plasticity in function of the subjective desires, without which the natural data of its biological configuration can constitute an ordinary normative reference, established by the customs or laws of society. In this way, those things previously considered to be perversions according to natural norms, are now considered to be part of a legitimate pluralism. The body desired and willed becomes the criterion for a remoulding of the physical body now considered to be neutral of meaning for acting. The body becomes a fully qualified "object" of technology, subject to the mind.

One of the most interesting points offered by Gidden's analysis

---

[64] Giddens, *The Transformation,* op.cit., p. 68.

[65] Ibid., p. 207.

[66] Ibid., p. 68.

[67] Ibid., p. 36.

is taken from the observation that "romantic love is the harbinger of the pure relationship, although it stands in tension with it".[68] It is certainly in tension insofar as it is based on a total asymmetry of the relationship and on a complete segregation of the experience of love from any calculation of reason. Romanticism renders l'*amour passion* absolute, considering it to be the very essence of love: an irrational event, outside of the possibility of wilful control or of institutional regulation.[69]

But starting precisely from here, the point in common between romantic love and the "pure" relationship also manifests itself: ultimately the criterion of validity in relation to love has been reduced to the subject himself of the affective and sexual experience, interpreted in a self-referential sense. Neither romantic love nor the "pure" relationship sees the sexually differentiated body in its intentional dynamic, according to which it is orientated toward the other person and arrives in this way at the origin of the event of love.

In both conceptions, intimacy is reduced to the subject's self-awareness and is exhausted in the experience of subjectivity: the body and affectivity which react to the exterior presence of the other. Absorbed by the intensity of feeling or enclosed in the seeking of one's own pleasure or the emotional advantage that the relationship can bring, the subject fails to recognize the foundation of the sexual and affective experience which enthrals him. Intimacy ultimately ends in the emptiness of the "pure relationship" in which the subject finds himself once again desolate and alone. The urges and affections which fulfilled him, instead of opening him to the reality of an encounter, now enclose him within himself, confirming his solitude.

It is also clear that the "pure relationship" is devoid of the idea of the communion of persons achievable through the sexually differentiated body and makes it impossible to consider the public relevance of love

---

[68] Ibid. p. 8.

[69] Cf. K.S. Pope, *On Love and Loving, Psychological Perspectives on the Nature and Experience of Romantic Love*, Jossey-Bass Publishers, San Francisco - Washington DC - London 1980.

as a "common good" of society.[70] The idea of democratic autonomy, applied to intimacy, makes the body a battlefield where the public and the private conflict. On the one hand, the idea of autonomy and the body's total manipulability lead to the claim of legitimacy for any manner of acting out of the "pure relationship", as if the state were obliged to accept the abandonment of every normative requirement in the sphere of intimacy; on the other hand, this transformation of intimacy is not neutral; it brings radical, social changes with repercussions for the whole of society.

At the end of his book, Giddens allows his awareness of the reductive character of a sexuality experienced as a "pure relationship" to show through as well as his nostalgia for that echo of transcendence which sexuality itself inevitably bears. However, this transcendence is denied in the modern transformation of intimacy in which it is uncoupled from the symbolic horizon bound to the cycle of generations. Here are his concluding words: "A civilization dedicated to sex is a society in which death has been deprived of meaning… In this perspective, sexuality is not the antithesis of a civilization dedicated to economic growth and to technical control, but rather the incarnation of its bankruptcy".[71]

The question concerning the interpretation of affective experience, which had already shown itself, re-emerges more strongly, precisely at this point: what is the meaning of corporeity and love in reference to intimacy? In the measure that a merely self-referential consciousness plunges into the void that separates love from the reality of the other and from society, it will be necessary to take up again the analysis of the experience of love so as to trace its origin and to rediscover elements that enable a different interpretation of intimacy. This seems to have been the precise intention of the reflection of John Paul II in his great catecheses on human love in the divine plan: he wants to return to the original experience of the encounter between man and woman and to illuminate it in its constitutive elements.

---

[70] In this regard, see the wisdom of J. Granados, "You are the light of the world". Mission of the Family, Small Domestic Church", *Anthropotes* (2008).

[71] Giddens, *The Transformation,* op.cit., p. 216.

2. The nuptial body and the original male / female difference

In order to approach this magisterial teaching, whose literary genre and complex structure are not easily explained,[72] it is useful to begin with a brief annotation concerning its methodological novelty. On the basis of the conversation between Jesus and the Pharisee concerning marriage (cf. *Mt* 19:3ff), the Pope declares his desire to return to the "beginning" of the love between man and woman, that is, to the "original truth, based on the authentically human experience".[73] Here, by "beginning", he is referring first of all to the revelation, contained in the book of Genesis, of God the Creator's original plan, who "created them male and female". But this plan is not only revealed in the Scriptures; it is also impressed in the body and in the heart of every man and woman. It even involves a return to the human experience of love. It is a "legitimate means of theological interpretation", says John Paul II, precisely because Christ the Redeemer confirms the gift of creation and guarantees the continuity and unity between man's states of life, before and after sin.[74] In this way, "beginning" also points to the original or elementary experience of love, considered within the essential and enduring elements of the phenomenological method.[75]

---

[72] In this regard, see: L. Ciccone, *Uomo-donna. L'amore umano nel piano divino. La grande Catechesi del mercoledì di Giovanni Paolo II*, Elledici, Leumann (To) 1986, pp. 11-23, who speaks to a certain extent about "catecheses" just as they are officially presented as "reflections" or even as "universal lectures". Recently, the Editor of the English edition has published the archival discovery of the *John Paul II Foundation*, care of *Dom Polski* of Rome, a typescript in Polish entitled "Man and woman he created them", prepared before the papal election of Karol Wojtyla. Other annotated manuscripts for the subdivision of the material of the corresponding Wednesday Catecheses have also been reported and effectively explained by: M. Waldstein, "New Textual Evidence for the Structure of John Paul II's Catecheses on Human Love", in *Anthropotes* XXI / 2 (2005), 271-276.

[73] John Paul II, op. cit., *Man and Woman He Created Them,* TOB 23, p. 218.

[74] Ibidem, 4, p. 142.

[75] As in: A. Scola, *L'esperienza elementare. La vena profonda del Magistero di Giovanni Paolo II*, Marietti, Genova 2003; M. Harper McCarthy, "L'amore sponsale alla luce dell'«esperienza elementare»", in L. Melina-S. Grygiel (Eds), *Amare l'amore umano. L'eredità di Giovanni Paolo II sul Matrimonio e la Famiglia*, Cantagalli, Siena 2007, pp. 129-147; L. Melina – J. Noriega – J.-J. Pérez-Soba, *Camminare nella luce dell'amore. I fondamenti della morale cristiana*, Cantagalli, Siena 2008, pp. 146-153.

That hermeneutic circularity between experience and revelation is such that it constitutes the characteristic and unique method of these catecheses. However, it is also based on a still more fundamental and Christological understanding of the term "beginning": Christ the Redeemer, risen in the flesh, is the "Beginning" in the light of which the human truth of experience and the theological truth of creation find their definitive clarification.

In the search for the original experience of love, there emerges firstly an attention to the reality of the body, which the Pope defines as the "primordial sacrament" or even the "sacrament of the person",[76] the visible sign of the invisible reality of the person. He is not concerned with an approach to this reality using the method of empirical science or the method of metaphysics, but with the phenomenological attitude that sees the body starting from the experience of the subject.[77] The contributions of science and metaphysics to the comprehension of human corporeity are certainly not refuted, but it is affirmed that for an adequate "theology of the body", it will be necessary to adopt the perspective of subjectivity and intersubjectivity, which alone is capable of seeing the whole richness of experience while avoiding a reductive objectification of the body.

Here, the reflections of John Paul II form a treasure and are crossbred with the analyses of the phenomenology of the body developed especially in the French environment.[78] The body is not just viewed from the outside but is understood from the inside to be something alive and living, not just as something that senses, but as something that senses its own sensing, as Merleau-Ponty would say. The specificity of the human body indeed consists in the fact that it not only perceives reality, but also perceives itself as the source of its own perception: "it sees itself seeing; it is touched by

---

[76] Op. cit., *Man and Woman He Created Them.* TOB 19, p. 201; TOB 87, p. 465; in this regard: J. Merecki, "Il corpo, sacramento della persona", in L. Melina – S. Grygiel (Eds), *Amare l'amore umano*, cit., pp. 173-185.

[77] Ibid., TOB 28, p. 198.

[78] In this regard, it suffices to mention the names of: G. Marcel, M. Merleau-Ponty, J.P. Sartre and M. Henry.

its own touching; it is visible and sensible to itself".[79] In this way, the experience of self-consciousness is opened at the same time, in which the subject emerges through contact with the reality of the other. Subjectivity is always in polar tension with regard to a reality to which it is intentionally orientated and which is presented as being other with regard to oneself. Paul Ricoeur, in the book, *Oneself as Other*, speaks of three areas of passivity or of otherness, by means of which the subject develops access to his own identity: the experience of the body, the encounter with the other person and the presence of conscience as the voice of the Other in me.[80]

The body is, first of all, the place of openness to reality, or better still the place which offers hospitality to reality which, touching the person, consults and provokes him. This primordial encounter with the world attests that he belongs, through the body, to the domain of the visible, although he also transcends it thanks to his awareness of his sensing. John Paul II affirmed in this regard that this original relationship to the world demonstrates that "man's corporeity itself belongs to the structure of the personal subject more profoundly than the fact that he is also masculine or feminine in his somatic constitution".[81] Corporeity does not totally coincide with sexuality, by which it has also and essentially been represented.

In effect, the experience, which on the basis of the book of Genesis comes to be called "original solitude", manifests the superiority of man as subject whether it is in confronting the visible world, which he dominates through his work, or with respect to the animals, with which he is unable to establish the reciprocity of a communion.[82] It is now through the body and not simply by his self-awareness that the man experiences solitude: therefore, solitude expresses the subjectivity of the body itself, which is not reducible to a merely material element of

[79] M. Merleau-Ponty, *L'occhio e lo spirito*, Studio editoriale, Milano 1989, n. 12, p. 18; cf. Also M. Henry, *Incarnazione. Una filosofia della carne,* Sei, Milano 2001, 183-190.

[80] Cf. P. Ricoeur, *Sé come un altro*, Jaca Book, Milano 2000, pp. 431-474. In English as: *Oneself as Other,* University of Chicago Press, 1992.

[81] Op. cit., *Man and Woman He Created Them.* TOB 8, p. 156.

[82] Ibid., TOB 6, p. 150.

the visible world. Here, we notice two other very important elements: first of all, it is through his actions that man becomes conscious of his body as subjectivity;[83] secondly, the foundation of this solitude is represented by the fact that man, because of what he is, is also, through his corporeity, constituted in a unique, exclusive and unrepeatable relationship with God himself: he is the "partner of the Absolute", since he is created "in the image of God".[84] Therefore, solitude in the world, on the one hand, expresses the experience of deficiency and dissatisfaction along with an incapacity for being adequately integrated into the visible reality in which he also participates; on the other hand, it manifests the transcendence of a call to go beyond, toward a sphere that remains, for the moment, hidden and disquieting.

The revelation of the enigma of solitude occurs, however, only in the encounter with the woman and it is precisely here that the revelation of the meaning of the body is given, together with the possibility of an authentic experience of intimacy. Certainly, it concerns a relationship with another, but it is a relationship of singular importance precisely because it is mediated by the flesh and experienced in it. "This is flesh of my flesh and bone of my bones" (*Gen* 2:23). It concerns, says the Pope, a second and definitive creation of man in the unity of two beings.[85] In an exact sense, this is the place where the complete subjectivity of man emerges: in the encounter with the other person of the opposite sex, and therefore through the mediation of the body.

But what is it about this unique encounter that is qualitatively different from the simple encounter with the visible world? Here body and person, nature and subjectivity really are intertwined. John Paul II offers an important analysis of "conjugal knowledge", by which two become "one flesh only", and this merits closer examination.[86]

He says that, in conjugal knowledge, man and woman are not only given to each other as objects defined by their body and sex

---

[83] Ibid., TOB 7, p. 153.

[84] Ibid., TOB 6, p. 150.

[85] Ibid., TOB 4, p. 142.

[86] Ibid., TOB 20, p. 204.

and therefore determined "by nature"; rather, they are given to each other as unique and unrepeatable subjects, that is, as persons. So it is in relationship with the woman that the body of the man manifests all his subjectivity and vice versa. The man/woman relationship is revealed to be the place where identity emerges. Inter-corporeity and not just intersubjectivity is the context in which personal identity is manifested.

The analysis of erotic perception which Maurice Merleau-Ponty developed in his *Phénomenologie de la perception* can be helpful for illustrating these annotations.[87] According to him, the erotic perception re-awakens the subject to himself, precisely because it opens his eyes to the other in a specific way: not as something that stands before me externally, but as an otherness that belongs to me because it is connatural to me and is "for me". It does not so much concern the perception of the sexual characteristics of the other's body as such, that is, of its genital organs, but a global perception of the body as subjectivity which evokes and reawakens one's own bodily subjectivity, beginning precisely with the sexual difference. However, the whole sexual dimension of the other can never be reduced to genital aspects. In explaining this, the French philosopher proposes the case of the young boy who has still not had sexual experience and who witnesses a scene of sexual activity from the outside; far from feeling himself to be involved in it, he experiences disgust. It is clear therefore that in erotic perception, the body of the other is pursued, since it attracts, not simply through its sexual characteristics, but through the personal encounter that it promises. This awareness overcomes the merely objective perception (*cogitatio*) of a given content (*cogitatum*) and symbolizes the intentional opening of one sexually differentiated body to another in a tension toward fulfilment. For Merleau-Ponty, this confirms subjectivity.

[87] M. Merleau-Ponty, *Fenomenologia della percezione*, Bompiani, Milano 2003, pp. 222-261. (in English as *Phenomenology of Perception,* Routledge, 2002, Trans. Colin Smith) I must draw attention to this text in the reading of a thesis of D. Donegà, *Il corpo e la sessualità in Maurice Merleau-Ponty. L'intenzionalità del corpo umano*, prepared under the direction of Prof. J. Noriega and consequently discussed in the Licentiate degree in June, 2007 at Rome, care of the Pontifical John Paul II Institute for Studies of Marriage and Family.

The phenomenological analysis therefore emphasizes the existence of a specific manner of relationship to one's own body and to the body of the other which reveals a new form of intimacy. Between the merely automatic reactions of the bio-physiological sphere of sexuality, constituted by the instincts and the objective intellectual representation determined by detached rational consideration, we find what Merleau-Ponty calls the "vital, immanent zone".[88] Here, the body's own intentionality is played out. It reacts to the presence of the other who is felt to be affectively significant insofar as his or her presence reawakens the body's subjectivity in correspondence with desire. The presence of the body of the other is perceived by me, the subject, to be enriching and filled with promise. Therefore, it is capable of mobilizing it in a tension toward a fuller union. Intimacy is no longer empty; a freely-given presence of the body-person of the other now dwells in it.

The *masculine/feminine* sexual difference is shown to be irreducible. It is not simply concerned with a distinct, natural configuration of the body at the biological level,[89] but with a complementary reciprocity, in which corporeal subjectivity itself is found to be differentiated (*dif-ferre*) in another form, which allows for the specific potential of unity in the flesh. It is within the erotic perception, in the reciprocal attraction of the sexually differentiated bodies, that this diversity appears as a good and promising difference indicative of an encounter which acquires a specific existential value because it promises a communion of persons.

The sexual connotation is not only a given of nature attested to by observation and as such liable to a plurality of anthropological interpretations, but provides evidence that in the erotic perception, it acquires a specific meaning in reference to the person. John Paul II calls it "spousal meaning",[90] indicating, in this way, the appeal for

---

[88] Ibid., p. 222.

[89] Cf. A. Scola, *Il mistero nuziale. I: Uomo-donna*, Pul-Mursia, Roma 2006, pp. 98-104 (In English: A. Scola, *The Nuptial Mystery*, Eerdmans Pub. Co., 2005); M. Chiodi, "La relazione uomo/donna come forma fondamentale della differenza", in *Teologia* 32 (2007), 11-35.

[90] Op. cit., *Man and Woman He Created Them,* TOB 14-18, pp. 181-198.

expressing, in and through the body, love for the other person, that is, the gift of self. Such meaning is rooted in the passivity of the body and therefore implies as its foundation an ontological openness to the other given by the Creator which can be called original communion.[91] Sexual difference assumes such relevance for freedom precisely through the experience of this original communion which also discloses the expectation that a more complete unity in the flesh between the persons might be constructed in practice. The body ceases in this way to be matter that can be moulded at will; sexuality is no longer presented in a neutral and ductile way, as a manipulable object at the disposition of the individual's free will. In the encounter with the sexually differentiated body of the other, one's own body is revealed to be nuptial and called to love.

3. The vocation to love

The experience of love is presented in Scripture, and not infrequently in classical literature,[92] as a "reawakening", as a release from the heavy torpor that weighs upon existence, condemning it to inertia. It is called, at the same time, to live in the light of a new presence and learns to recognize a horizon of meaning, summoning us to a way that leads to fulfilment. This reawakening also implies wonder and the assumption of responsibility: it is no longer possible to live in a dream. In this sense, sexuality is dramatic and possesses existential value. It promises escape from the anonymous life of the body, with its complexity of vital functions, to the beginning of a truly personal life involving personal choices. It is again Merleau-Ponty who observes: from the moment that sexuality involves the body as "the form of its very being", it implies the elaboration of a general manner of life.[93] The outcome is therefore "dramatic because we commit the whole of our

[91] Cf. John Paul II, Apostolic Letter, *Mulieris dignitatem*, n. 7; M. Nédoncelle, *La réciprocité des consciences. Essai sur la nature de la personne*, Aubier-Montaigne, Paris 1942, 10-47.

[92] It suffices by way of example to recall by way of introduction the work of Dante dedicated to his own amorous experience: "The New Life – La vita nuova".

[93] M. Merleau-Ponty, *Phenomenology*, op. cit., pp. 232-234.

personal life to one another",[94] risking its entire meaning.

The main themes of freedom emerge here, namely: its dialogical character and its gradual fulfilment through acting. It is concerned, as we have seen, with themes which, on the one hand, were removed by the romantic interpretation of love, and which, on the other, were taken up by the contemporary vision of "pure love" in the form of a contraposition that ends up objectifying the sexually differentiated body. The great catecheses of John Paul II take these up in the perspective of a vocation to love[95] that illumines the way of integration.

"The body, in its masculinity and femininity, has been given as a task to the human spirit", in such a way that it increasingly becomes a sign of the person and can in this way express and achieve its spousal meaning.[96] The spiritualization of the body does not indicate a negation of its instinctive or affective dynamics; rather it points to their personal integration in view of the gift. John Paul II noted that in St Paul the dynamic contraposition between the "flesh" and the "spirit" is not equivalent to the anthropological dualism between body and soul or between spirit and matter.[97]

Above all, the body expresses the irreducible presence of personal freedom in the experience of love. The freely given event and encounter with the other does not just involve persons passively but also through their natural dynamisms. Indeed, "by the very fact of being man and woman, each has been 'given' to the other as a unique and unrepeatable subject, as an 'I', that is, as a person".[98] This is because sex does not just decide man's somatic individuality; it also defines his personal and concrete identity, which he is called to fulfil in a communion of persons. Eros acquires, in this way, a destiny: the *telos* which constitutes the axle that bears the weight of action is given

---

[94] Ibid., p. 240.

[95] Op. cit., *Man and Woman He Created Them.* TOB 46, p. 309.

[96] Ibid., TOB 59, p. 360.

[97] In this regard: A.J. Walker, «"Sown Psychic, Raised Spiritual": the Lived Body as the Organ of Theology», in *Communio (USA)* 33 (Summer 2006), 203-215.

[98] Op. cit., *Man and Woman He Created Them.* TOB 20, p. 204.

within the affective dynamic itself, avoiding in this way an intrinsically intellectualistic understanding.[99] If the body reveals the person, the encounter of bodies challenges persons in their radical capacity to receive the other.

Freedom emerges precisely in response to the person as other, who becomes present in the sphere of intimacy through the awakening of the bodily and affective dynamisms toward the other which drives the subject toward that communion which is the profound reason for the fascination of the sexual encounter. It is neither contra-posed to the natural dynamic of instinct directed toward the sexual qualities of the body nor reduced to them. Rather, it orientates them in the direction of the fulfilment of the person whose *sexually differentiated* body is sacramental. From the point of view of the interior dynamic, freedom is not therefore born out of emptiness. Instead, it assumes the dynamic urges of the body and, through affectivity, dimensions them in the context of an appropriate relationship with the other person. From the ontological point of view, freedom is a response to the gift of a primary presence of the other. It is a consent to being, which, precisely by preceding it, calls it forth.

In this way, the presence of an original love also comes to light. It precedes both the persons involved and their gift to each other. It is the ultimate foundation of their goodness and the guarantee of the promise that their encounter discloses. At the end of his volume dedicated to the erotic phenomenon, J.-L. Marion acknowledges this very point: "The experience of eros requires that another lover precedes me and makes his plea to me in silence".[100] In this way, the logic of human love, by being realistically situated in relation to the original love of God, cannot be equivocal or merely unambiguous, but must accept the fundamental analogy that derives from the fact that man is responsive by nature and able to subsist only by recognizing,

[99] Cf. J. Noriega, *Il destino dell'eros. Prospettive di morale sessuale*, EDB, Bologna 2006.

[100] J.-L. Marion, *Le phénomène érotique Six méditations, Grasset*, Paris 2003, p. 331. In reality, Marion does not recognize then the analogical character of love: cf. J.-J. Pérez-Soba, "La logica, analogica dell'amore", in N. Reali (Ed.), *L'amore, tra filosofia e teologia. In dialogo con Jean-Luc Marion*, Lup, Roma 2007, 155-170.

at least implicitly, the primacy of that original love.

The category of vocation, introduced in the catecheses within the theme of love, indicates that the Pope's concern is to achieve a sense of the ongoing task of love which involves the gradual unfolding of freedom. He is concerned with the passage of love from its experience as a gratuitous event to the human act of love which is the achievement of a life-long task. He considers it to be especially necessary to avoid the romantic reduction of love to its initial, aesthetic moment, that is, to the moment of fascination which the encounter with the other occasions.

The affective dimension, if it is not thwarted in its dynamism but is orientated toward the other person, necessarily involves the goods that promote communion. As St Thomas Aquinas observed, "Love consists precisely in this: in wanting the good for the beloved".[101] The weakness of so many personalistic reflections consists precisely in their being incapable of integrating the objective element of the good into the relationship between persons, particularly, into the relationship between man and woman and therefore reducing interpersonality to intersubjectivity.[102] In reality, the intersubjective relationship is impossible without a communication between subjects and this in turn points to the objective nature of the good. Without the communication of objective goods, the person becomes a mere postulate devoid of content.[103]

[101] 'In hoc precipue consistit amor, quod amans amato bonum velit': Tommaso d'Aquino, *Summa contra gentiles*, III, 90, ed. T.S. Centi, ESD, Bologna 2001, p. 337. See in this regard: J.-J. Pérez-Soba, *"Amor es nombre de persona" Estudio de la interpersonalidad en el amor en Santo Tomás de Aquino*, Pul-Mursia, Roma 2000.

[102] In this regard: J.-J. Pérez-Soba, *La pregunta por la persona, la respuesta de la interpersonalidad. Estudio de una categoría personalista,* Facultad de Teología San Dámaso, Madrid 2004; G. Mazzocato "Il tema del corpo nel rinnovamento personalista della morale sessuale", in *Teologia* 25 (2000), 50-70; Id. "L'indirizzo personalista e i suoi problemi", in G. Angelini (Ed.), *La legge naturale. I principi dell'umano e la molteplicità delle culture*, Glossa, Milano 2007, pp. 151-185.

[103] Maurice Nédoncelle is clear on this topic: '...a person who, in one way or another fails to progress to the school of objectivity, becomes intolerable (...) A communion of consciousness, except in fugitive experiences, is achieved on earth through communication, that is, by means of common action that sets in the same amalgam, an awareness which is given, the nature that shares values and the thought that mediates them.', in *Conscience et logos. Horizons et méthodes d'une philosophie personaliste*, Éd. de l'Épi, Paris 1960, p. 40.

The vocational perspective to which love opens the person involves consideration of the dimension of time and of the practical mediation required in vocational achievement: it is a complex passage from desire to the gift of self and from initial emotion in the presence of the beloved to acting in favour of a communion of persons. Here, a hiatus emerges with the attempt to adequately interpret the personal dimension of love and, in particular, the link between affectivity and the gift of self. This is evident in the scholastic explanation of the human act, which fragments it into numerous partial acts of the various faculties.[104] The particular goods, which mediate the communion between persons, become relevant in the corporeal and affective dimensions precisely in relation to the fullness of a vocation to love. The theoretical model of an "anthropology of the faculties"[105] can be surpassed if the personal value of the act is recognized, above all the dynamic unity which constitutes it in the strength of love. Love establishes the intrinsic, personal value of action, which has special need of the moment of truth, given by reason, so that it may become a reality. In all of this, the affective dynamic has special relevance thanks to its capacity to unify the dynamics of action between the lover and the beloved.

In this light, it is possible to catch a glimpse of the path along which the thought of Karol Wojtyła matured, a path which preceded and prepared for his papal *Catecheses*. His first work on *Love and Responsibility*, which dated back to 1960, and which was treated in the first chapter of this volume, still reflects a scholastic understanding of acting with its fragmentary approach of the various faculties. However, his psychological considerations and his personalistic emphasis already

---

[104] We are referring to the classic subdivision established by Billuart. For this, see: J. Romiti, *De processu evolutivo doctrinae de actu humano completo in operibus S. Thomae Aquinatis*, PUG, Milano 1949. S. Pinckaers introduces a new interpretation of St Thomas theory of action in a dynamic and unitary perspective, "La structure de l'acte humain suivant saint Thomas", in *Revue Tomiste* 55 (1955), 393-413. On the whole question, see: J.-J. Pérez-Soba, "L'amore ci fa pensare", in J.-J. Pérez-Soba-L. Granados (Ed.), *Il logos dell'agape: amore e ragione come principi dell'agire*, Cantagalli, Siena 2008.

[105] For a critique of the anthropological model of the faculties and an alternative proposal based on the dramatic model suggested by the biblical tradition, see G. Angelini, *Eros e agape. Oltre l'alternativa*, Glossa, Milano 2006, pp. 23ff, 32ff., 63-67.

urge him toward a more intimate unification of the act. In particular, the influence accorded to the "great and strong emotions", which he emphasizes, allows for the integration of the instinctive and affective dimensions in the perspective of personal love. The later philosophical work, *The Acting Person* of 1969, enabled the introduction of a dynamic and unified perspective of the acting subject, who perfects himself precisely through his acting.[106] In this work, which combines a phenomenological approach with a metaphysical interpretation, the act is seen as a stage in the self-realization of the person, not as the expression of a single faculty. Although the *Catechesis* on human love cannot be considered to be a text that attempts to confront the issue of human action systematically, his earlier theoretical acquisitions are further reflected on and developed in it, particularly with their emphasis on affectivity and its integration with the personalistic dimension. This is achieved through the meditation of the spousal meaning of the body and the "consciousness" movement toward becoming "one flesh".

4. The Language of the body and acts of love

The topic of the necessary practical mediation of love is dealt with in the catecheses where John Paul II introduces his original argument in favour of the "language of the body",[107] which he defines as the substrate and content of the sacramental sign of the communion of spouses. We are then in the context of the anthropological presuppositions of sacramental acting and precisely in the problematic of its truth and efficacy. In order to grasp the meaning of the language of the body, we must first consider it in the context of the communication between subjects, who "communicate precisely on the basis of the 'common union' existing between them so as to achieve or express a

[106] It is necessary here to refer also to the important 1974 article, "Il problema del costituirsi della cultura attraverso la "praxis" umana", now in K. Wojtyla, *Metafisica della persona. Tutte le opere filosofiche e saggi integrativi* (Eds G. Reale and T. Styczen), Bompiani, Milano 2003, pp. 1447-1461.

[107] Op. cit., *Man and Woman He Created Them.* TOB 103, p. 531.

reality that pertains only to the sphere of the subject-person".[108]

We find two levels of meaning mentioned here: one is perennial; the other is unique and unrepeatable. The first concerns the "objective sense" of which the body is not the author – rather, it has been "spoken by the word of the living God";[109] the second is "subjective" and man is the author of it by means of his necessary and continuous "re-reading" of the original truth. The Pope observes that in this re-reading, "something more" occurs: man becomes the "co-author", with God, of the language of the body, taking up again and consenting to the original meanings that are characteristic of creation. As a result, not everything in the language of love can be creative: in the experience of love, corporeal gestures are given which have an intrinsic and non-manipulable meaning.[110] In this sense, to say that "the body speaks" expresses an *analogia attributionis (analogy of attribution)*: the subject of the discourse is man himself who, as male and female, "consents to the body by speaking for it".[111] It connects, therefore, with the possibility granted to man to be a co-author, and to express himself truly or falsely.

Along with the theme of the language of the body, two related points are worthy of explanation. The first concerns the "prophetism of the body":[112] a prophet is one who expresses in human words a truth that comes from God. The body too needs to discern the divine voice. But it is interesting here to observe how this voice makes itself known. It is not discovered in the objective considerations of the physical qualities of the body nor in the metaphysical interpretations of its ontological finality, but in the sphere of the communication between subjects – persons. It is in this context that the biological functions become relevant: the desires, instincts and affective orientations which make up human sexuality.

---

108 Ibid., TOB 7, p. 153.

109 Ibid., TOB 104 and 105, pp. 534-542.

110 Which has the value of a fundamental critique of the work of A. Guindon, *The Sexual Creators. An Ethical Proposal for Concerned Christians*, University Press of America, Lanham-New York-London 1986.

111 Ibid., TOB 106, p. 542.

112 Ibid., TOB 104, p. 534.

The second point concerns the practical character of language: it is not just concerned with expressing something, but with pronouncing words that have a performative value because they achieve what they say: they modify the personal reality of each person and they influence the relationship between the persons involved. The sacramental context, on which the reflection on the language of the body is established, suggests such a reflection concerning action. In other words, the meaning of the body is not just conceptual; it is lived concretely and as such determines man's history. "We, in these analyses, – affirms John Paul II – have always taken account of man's historicity".[113]

It becomes clear therefore that it is impossible to interpret acts of sexual love in a reductive way as though they were mere gestures expressive of personal consciousness.[114] To act is not just to manifest meaning implicitly; it also achieves its meaning and only in its achievement does one become conscious of the meaning that springs from action. Subjective identity lies in the ebb and flow between action and consciousness.[115] Maurice Blondel has shown with great clarity that the primacy of praxis consists precisely in this.[116] Yet the mystery of action cannot find its definitive hermeneutic only in reference to the dialectic between *volonté voulante* and *volonté voulue (*that is, between the profound aspiration of being and any concrete determination of the good in a particular decision*)* and the dynamic of desire. The catecheses of John Paul II show how action is meaningfully constituted in the context of love, that is, in the concrete dynamic of the nuptial body, which, through affectivity, is intentionally orientated toward the

[113] Ibidem, TOB 31, p. 253.

[114] G. Mazzocato's critique seems worthy of mention here concerning the interpretation of sexuality as a language proposed by X. Lacroix: G. Mazzocato, "L'indirizzo personalista", Op. cit., 177-179, which refers to X. Lacroix, *Il corpo di carne. La dimensione etica, estetica e spirituale dell'amore*, EDB, Bologna 1996, pp. 111-128.

[115] Cf. F.G. Brambilla, "Il corpo alla prova dei manuali di antropologia teologica", in Associazione Teologica Italiana, *Il corpo alla prova dell'antropologia cristiana* (Ed. R. Repole), Glossa, Milano 2007, pp. 147-185.

[116] Cf. M. Blondel, *L'Action (1893). Essai d'une critique de la vie et d'une science de la pratique*, Presses Universitaires de France, Paris 1973. See also the English translation by Olivier Blanchette, Action (1893): *Essay on a critique of life and a science of practice*, Notre Dame, Indiana, 2007.

reality of the other. Furthermore, in the interpersonal relationship, action is shown to be founded on original love.

The human being and, in particular, his sexual experience which is so significant for configuring his life's meaning, cannot be resolved in the social dimension of language and just absorbed into the relativism of the ever changing interpretations of history. Through the body, he is opened to the reality of the other as subject and to the world of objects, and this constitutes the irreducible polarity of his acting.

Starting from its nuptiality, the body also speaks of its origin and its potential fruitfulness, that is, of its generational penetration of existence by which it finds itself in the cycle of life and death. In this way, the *sexually differentiated* body invites the person to recognize himself as "son" or "daughter" and to embrace the vocation to "fatherhood" or "motherhood". This clearly implies the insertion of intimacy into the sphere of social life. For this reason, it is preferable to speak of the body as "nuptial" rather than as "spousal": indeed, nuptiality is a richer and more complete concept, inasmuch as, by referring etymologically to the definitive insertion of spouses into the family home, it does not merely imply an orientation to being a husband or wife, but also to becoming a father, mother or even a child.[117]

The reference to paternity/maternity and to filiation enables us to see how sexuality is open to transcendence, which renders it irreducible to mere desire, to subjective sentiment or to the undermining forces in society. Welcoming a child, who is never merely desired, willed or produced, is always like welcoming a guest who "comes from afar"[118], and returns to God by a new way, the way of original love from which every paternity in heaven and on earth takes its name (cf. *Eph* 3:14). It now becomes clear how human love, fully lived in all of its dimensions, joins with God's original love by collaborating with it and pursuing it with creative action.

[117] For this determination, see: A. Scola, "Il mistero nuziale,. Originarietà e fecondità", in *Anthropotes* XXIV/1 (2008). For the etymological references of "spouse" and of "marriage" see: M. Cortellazzo - M.A. Cortellazzo (Ed.), *Il nuovo etimologico. Deli Dizionario Etimologico della Lingua Italiana*, Zanichelli, Bologna 1999, respectively, p. 1594 and p. 1050.

[118] Cf. G. Angelini, *Il figlio. Una benedizione, un compito*, Vita e pensiero, Milano 1991.

Precisely by its being rooted in the body, the language of the body overcomes the self-referencing tendency both of individual and of shared, social consciousness and turns the person outwards towards the fullness of reality. Margaret S. Archer has stated that, between the partial explanation of neurobiology and the interpretative understanding of sociology is "the 'middle ground' of the practical life, in which our emerging characteristics and potentialities distance themselves from our biological origins and prepare us for social development".[119] Language is not born in the void of consciousness but is rooted in the ontic structure of the person, which it reflects. It is precisely in the tension of affectivity toward the other and in the perspective of a good life that gesture acquires its meaning and can be evaluated in its capacity to adequately express love.

This interpretation of human praxis makes it possible to articulate the nexus of the reciprocal correlation between nature and culture.[120] Culture is the inescapable context in which acts and words, including the language of the body, are inserted and which are intended to express and attain love. It offers a primary interpretation of nature, which helps to humanize the human act by interpreting its meaning. However, it must, in its turn, be applied to the original and elementary experiences in which the truth of love is manifested. Again, Merleau-Ponty, in stating that the lived body is transcendent with respect to the biological body, affirms the connection that is established between "natural" and "cultural": "Behaviours create meanings that transcend anatomy but are nevertheless immanent to behaviour as such since it is communicated and understood".[121]

It is possible, at this point, to insert the theme of "purity" (which is so ignored today) into the discussion of sexual morality. John Paul II had the courage and wisdom to treat the topic of purity extensively

---

[119] M.S. Archer, *Essere umani. Il problema dell'agire*, Marietti 1820, Genova – Milano 2007, 271.

[120] Cf. G. Angelini, "La legge naturale e il ripensamento dell'antropologia", in G. Angelini (Ed.), *La legge naturale*, cit., 187-215.

[121] M. Merleau-Ponty, *Fenomenologia*, Op. cit., 261.

in his Catecheses.[122] It is treated in its practical capacity, which enables the person to act in a certain manner in cooperation with a special gift of the Holy Spirit. Furthermore, it concerns both virtue and charismatic gift in an operative synergy of human freedom and grace. Incidentally, the topic of virtue is entirely adequate in the context of culture. If culture points to what makes man more human, to what makes him grow in his humanity,[123] then a culture of the human person is achieved precisely in the virtues and springs anew through action linked to freedom and the gift of the Holy Spirit.

Purity is a capacity, "centred on the dignity of the body, that is, on the dignity of the person in relation to his body: to the femininity or masculinity manifested in this body".[124] It achieves victory over disunity and enables the person to express the gift of self in the body. Far from opposing the body and its dynamics, it sees its full value in reference to the vocation to love. In this way, it is an interior transformation which enables full transparency in the acts of the body: "it is the glory of the human body before God. It is the glory of God in the human body".[125]

Conclusion

Let us return, by way of conclusion, to the question posed at the beginning of this chapter. The controversy over the body led us back to a more radical question concerning the meaning of sexual intimacy. The modern conception of the sexual relationship as a "pure relationship", the latest outcome of the romantic interpretation of love, confronted us with the idea of an empty intimacy. The self-referencing tendency of consciousness encloses the individual in

---

[122] Op. cit., *Man and Woman He Created Them.* TOB 54-58, pp. 342-359. The classic treatment is by D. von Hildebrand, *In Defense of Purity*, Franciscan Herald Press, Chicago, 1970.

[123] Cf. John Paul II, *Discorso all'Unesco*, 2 June, 1980, cf. L. Negri, *L'uomo e la cultura nel magistero di Giovanni Paolo II*, Cseo-Saggi, Bologna 1983; F. Follo (ed.), *Jean-Paul II et la culture contemporaine*, Cerf, Paris 2005.

[124] Op. cit., *Man and Woman He Created Them,* TOB 56, p. 349.

[125] Ibidem, TOB 57, p. 352.

the pretext of a manipulative power over his own body and in the democratic claim of a contractual relationship with the other. If intimacy is empty, then the male-female difference remains exterior and conveys no meaning; it must be reabsorbed by freedom which is neither limited nor threatened. By leaving the restrictive horizon of an unconvincing subjectivism, it seems that merely returning to a naturalistic comprehension of the body, based on the empirical sciences, or to a metaphysical reading of it, neither explores nor points to the essential finalities.

The catecheses of John Paul II on human love in the divine plan have pointed out the way of return to the "beginning", that is, to the original experience fulfilled in the light of the biblical revelation. The analysis of the encounter between man and woman, experienced in the flesh, and that of the erotic perception which it involves, has enabled the intentional character of affective experience to emerge with great clarity. Starting from the gift of a primary, interior presence, it leads to a more complete encounter with the reality of the other. If intimacy is experienced in the affective presence of the other, then his interior presence is an invitation to a communion of persons. This reveals the abundance of the polarity of the body which opens it to the world and calls it, by acting, to fulfilment in the temporal and historical dimension.

The approach has turned out to be fruitful both for anthropology and for morality, since it has shown that the return to original experience and recognition of the affective dynamic that it involves enables the body's meanings to be rediscovered, no longer as extrinsically imposed on freedom, but as essential vectors of the dynamism of love. In this love, freedom can be attained. In this light, the body is revealed to be nuptial and to be called to love.

3
Man-Woman: the Archetype of Love according to Benedict XVI

The inaugural Encyclical of Pope Benedict XVI's pontificate is intentionally dedicated to the very centre of the Christian faith, to what constitutes its essence, namely: the image of God offered by Revelation (*Deus caritas est*) and the image of man and his way to God. The central affirmation of the document, taken from the first Letter of St John, namely: "God is love" (*1 Jn* 4:16), immediately won widespread approval, but perhaps so immediately that it could also be mistaken. Could such approval involve, paradoxically, the risk of diluting the meaning and compromising the identity of Christianity? In the cultural context in which we find ourselves, such a general consensus around the idea of God as love, can be accompanied by an attitude of intolerance toward the doctrinal and moral content of the Christian faith and toward its ecclesiastical form; furthermore, it can reveal a tendency to reduce it to a purely interior and invisible religion, deprived of any true reference to Christ.[126]

A widespread mentality favours an emotive concept of faith which is separated from reason and reduced, therefore, to an irrational and privatized option for faith. This option is associated with the romantic interpretation of affectivity. If believing is a purely subjective, interior event, then love also becomes a sentiment extraneous to reason and enclosed in individual consciousness. According to this vision, faith and love can be reduced to a private sphere of existence devoid of relevance for society's edification. Therefore, society will opt for the objectivity of scientific thought and for a contractual regulation of

[126] For this analysis, see: G. Angelini, *Eros e agape. Oltre l'alternativa,* Glossa, Milan, 2006, pp. 3-17.

justice between contra-posed interests. It is precisely to overcome this reductive interpretation of love, along with its consequent, erroneous understanding of the very nucleus of Christian faith, that Pope Benedict XVI, through his Encyclical, speak to us of the intrinsic logic of love.[127]

"So we know and believe in the love God has for us" (*1 Jn* 4:16). This is the hermeneutical key that prevents misunderstanding: the centre of the Christian faith is precisely that love which is neither an ethical decision nor a great idea but the encounter with an event, with a Person, namely: Jesus Christ, who has given life a new horizon and a decisive direction (*DCE* 1). Love, which is the very heart of the Christian life, is a response to that love which God first had for us and which he manifested in Christ. Apart from this, we would not really know what love is and could therefore be entirely mistaken about it.

1. The Archetype of the Nuptial Mystery

What is the image of God and of man that emerges from the Christian Revelation of love? What is the starting point for understanding it? By reflecting on the great semantic variety that language attributes to the word love, Benedict XVI affirms that "Amid this multiplicity of meanings, however, one in particular stands out: love between *man and woman*, where body and soul are inseparably joined and human beings glimpse an apparently irresistible promise of happiness. *This would seem to be the very epitome [archetype] of love*; all other kinds of love immediately seem to fade in comparison" (*DCE* 2).[128] To avoid error,

[127] Cf. J.J. Pérez-Soba Diez del Corral, "Una nuova apologetica: la testimonianza dell'amore. L'enciclica *Deus caritas est* di Benedetto XVI", in *Anthropotes* XXII/1 (2006), 145-169. In this respect, see also: L. Melina, C. Anderson (ed.), *La vía del amor. Reflexiones sobre la encíclica* Deus caritas est *de Benedicto XVI,* Monte Carmelo, Pontifical John Paul II Institute for Studies on Marriage and Family, Burgos, 2006.

[128] Translator's note: in the original Italian text of this compact volume, *Imparare ad amare alla scuola di Giovanni Paolo II e Benedetto XVI,* the author takes the heading of this section from the Italian of *DCE 2* which describes the love between man and woman as the "archetipo" of Christian love. The English translation uses the word "epitome" instead of "archetype".

it is necessary to begin with the love between man and woman, a love certainly characterized by eros, but which God himself has needed in order to reveal in spousal terms his *agapic* love toward the Chosen People.

The statement according to which the love between man and woman is the archetypical form of love is bold and immediately raises a number of opposing arguments. Nevertheless, it is the centre of Christian anthropology. On the one hand, the problem of spiritualism is opposed to such an affirmation; it distrusts the proposal of the love between man and woman as the model of every love, precisely because of the inescapability of sexuality in such love. According to the spiritualistic view, sexuality compromises the transcendence and gratuity of the loftier forms of love. It especially seems inappropriate to associate such love with divine love. Surely, agape, the fruit of grace, which is founded on faith and characterized by oblation, could have nothing in common with eros which is so related to the body, arising as it does from the desire to possess and orientated to self-affirmation. The protestant contraposition between eros and agape, codified in the famous study of Anders Nygren,[129] recommends an initial reserve toward the proposal to make the love between man and woman the archetype of every love.

This reserve also seems to be confirmed by a rejection that springs from another quarter and which is quite bound to contemporary gender theories. These claim to emancipate sexuality from the natural determinations of the body, even to the point of dissolving the identifying significance of the sexual difference between man and woman.[130] In this view, to make the love between man and woman an archetype of every kind of love is equivalent to subordinating the creative freedom of individuals to the slavery of their bodies. Democratic equality demands recognition of the right to treat one's own body with total plasticity, which includes, at the sexual level, the "pure" relationship explained in the previous chapter. "Pure" in

[129] A. Nygren, *Eros e agape. La nozione cristiana dell'amore e le sue trasformazioni*, Il Mulino, Bologna 1971.

[130] For a panorama of a socio-cultural kind: A. Giddens, *The Transformation of Intimacy: sexuality, love and eroticism in modern societies,* Stanford University Press, CA, USA, 1993.

this sense is certainly not related to chastity; rather it means being independent of any form of relationship imposed as a given by nature or culture and, therefore, not springing from the free choice of the individual.

We can easily see, even linguistically, that a common denominator unites these two currents of thought, despite their being so contraposed to our sensibility and at odds in their purposes: they both disregard the body which, in the case of puritan spiritualism, is denied in favour of a spiritual love, while in the case of the libertinism of gender theory, it is reduced to manipulable matter for the sake of pleasure. A kind of individualism is associated with this which, precisely because it refuses to recognize the intrinsic meaning of the body, fails to understand that it mediates the person in relationships as a constitutive dimension of his being.

The course chosen by Pope Benedict for his hermeneutical explanation begins with the concrete experience of love which at first is neither a thought nor a decision but an event of love in one's own life. As we shall see, such an event has a twofold reference: firstly, the love which arises between man and woman, but secondly, and especially, the advent of Christ who reveals and communicates the love of the Father. This involves overcoming rationalism and voluntarism. Let us try to follow, in our reflection, the points suggested by these words of the Encyclical, applying them firstly to the love between man and woman then allowing them to be illuminated by the Christian event. In what sense, therefore, does the love between man and woman become the concrete experience which is the archetype for understanding love? To speak of an event in this regard is to point to a new light which appears in love and involves the person, opening him to a fullness of meaning concerning the whole of existence which, as happens between people, takes the shape of an encounter. That is to say, it takes the form of an unforeseen and irreducible act that puts two freedoms into play.

In the case of sexuality, it concerns an event that is never totally controllable and always leads us beyond, to a sacred and unknown world, toward a greater and more mysterious encounter. This involves soul and body, freedom and affectivity, in the particularity of a new, intentional tension that orientates the lover toward the beloved: love searches for the fulfilment, in a real unity between persons, of that promise which the encounter has awakened from the beginning, causing the heart to shine resplendent with a perspective that is certainly pleasing and fascinating, but also mysterious and terrible insofar as it remains unknown. Paul Ricoeur has pointed out that "sexuality remains fundamentally impermeable to reflection and inaccessible to human control...Finally, when two beings embrace, they know not what they do, they know not what they want, they know not what they seek and they know not what they find. What is the meaning of this desire which drives one toward the other?"[131] Sexuality cannot be reabsorbed perfectly in concepts, nor be adequately resolved in ethics; in itself, it implies something sacred and can only be symbolically represented. It reveals something of the mystery of being itself and introduces us to it. What does eros speak to us about? What does it lead us to?

The body itself, in its living opening to the body of the other person, bears witness to that mystery of love which constitutes the foundation and destiny from which we come and towards which we are called to go, if we are to find our fulfilment. Precisely in the body, the original structure of love is revealed, that is, the transcendent dimension present in any kind of love, from the lowest and most vulgar to the noblest and most elevated.[132] Angelo Scola, starting from a reflection on John Paul II's *theology of the body* and the thought of Hans Urs von Balthasar, defined this original structure with the expression "nuptial mystery". In order to describe its characteristics, he traced it back, etymologically, to the ancient Romans' use of the veil for women who, after simple promises, became wives (*nuptae*) and were then carried to the marriage bed in view of their becoming

---

[131] P. Ricoeur, "La merveille, l'errance, l'énigme", in *Esprit* n. 289 (1960), 1665-1676.

[132] Cf. A. Scola, "Il mistero nuziale. Originarietá e fecunditá", in *Anthropotes* XXIII/2 (2007), in process of publication. For a more systematic study, see the following work by the same author: *Il mistero nuziale. 1: Uomo-Donna*, Pul-Mursia, Roma 1998; (*The Nuptial Mystery*, Eerdmans Publishing Co., 2005); *Il mistero nuziale: una prospettiva di teologia sistematica*, Lateran University Press, Rome 2003.

mothers. Nuptiality therefore implies not only the spousal relationship between man and woman, but also an orientation toward family, by means of paternity and maternity. The word "nuptial" is also related, as the word suggests, to "*nubes*"; to the clouds which hide but also reveal the heavens, filtering its light. Therefore, in the nuptial mystery, something of the transcendent mystery of love is revealed, that mystery which dwells in heaven and from heaven is reflected in the love between man and woman. As Pope Benedict affirms: "There is a certain relationship between love and the Divine: love promises infinity, eternity – a reality far greater and totally other than our everyday existence" (*DCE* 5).

The nuptial mystery, observed in the man-woman archetype, presents in this inseparable way, the unity of three constitutive factors which only in the fact of being contemporaneously given offer their integral fullness, namely: sexual difference, the reciprocal gift of self, and fruitfulness. The living body is always situated and orientated by the sexual difference in relation to the person of the opposite sex. The difference (*di-ferre*), in effect, indicates that its very humanity is communicated to the other in a new and complementary way. United to me and for me, there is another way of being "man", a way that is inaccessible, but complementary to me; a way that is unknown by its difference and fascinating on account of the reciprocity which it promises.

Therefore, the difference inscribed in the body is a vocation, a call to an opening and a communion of persons in the unity of their bodies, from the moment in which the body always implies the totality of the person and of persons.[133] John Paul II, in his catecheses on human love in the divine plan, coined a strong expression, saying that the body is the "sacrament of the person", a visible sign of the interior and invisible reality.

The asymmetric character of the reciprocity between man and woman, thanks to which there is never a complete and definitive fusion, even in the most intimate unity, demands that the relationship

[133] We must refer here to the "theology of the body" elaborated by John Paul II, *Man and woman he created them. A theology of the body*, Pauline Books and Media, Boston, 2006.

always remain open to a further exuberance of the gift exchanged which encounters in the procreation of a child, at the same time its fruit and testimony. As von Balthasar affirmed, "The union of two persons in one flesh, and the fruit of this union, must be considered together, despite the distance of time".[134] Fruitfulness specifically manifests the spiritual character of this relationship of one-flesh unity which the sexual difference makes possible: in effect, the fruit of the conjugal act is not just another example of the species, but a new personal subject who is pro-created in collaboration with the Creator.[135] "I have gotten a man with the help of the Lord" (*Gn* 4:1) is the cry, full of pride and fear, of the first mother who procreates. The "pro" indicates the beyond from where the child always comes, which cannot be reduced to just the father and mother. "For this reason I bow my knees before the Father, from whom every family in heaven and on earth is named" (*Eph* 3:14). The nuptial mystery, contemplated starting from the man-woman archetype, brings us to the threshold of original love, of which it is the image.

2. The Analogy of Love

The Encyclical of Pope Benedict offers us in this regard a second statement which is worth our dwelling on:

> From the standpoint of creation, *eros* directs man towards marriage, to a bond which is unique and definitive; thus, and only thus, does it fulfill its deepest purpose. *Corresponding to the image of a monotheistic God is monogamous marriage.* Marriage based on exclusive and definitive love becomes the icon of the relationship between God and his people and vice versa. God's way of loving becomes the measure of human love. This close connection between *eros* and marriage in the Bible has practically no equivalent in extra-biblical literature (*DCE* 11).

In this passage which is crucial for grasping the message of the

[134] H.U. von Balthasar, *La preghiera contemplativa*, Jaca Book, Milan 1982, p. 89.
[135] Cf. J. Ratzinger, "Uno sguardo teologico sulla procreazione umana", in *La via della fede. Le ragioni dell'etica nell'epoca presente*, Ares, Milan 1996, pp. 133-151.

Encyclical, the question of love is intimately bound to the question of God: by inverting the analogical reference, God's manner of loving is presented as the key and fundamental measure for understanding the essence of human love. At the same time, the question of marriage becomes decisive not only from the anthropological point of view, as the authentic destiny of eros defines,[136] but also from the theological point of view, as the authentic face of God reflects and testifies. If authentic conjugal love is achieved, the glory of God is given, but if its face is disfigured by denying the unicity and definiteness which are proper to marriage, then the face of God also becomes indiscernible.

Clearly, the connection between monotheism and monogamy referred to here is not a general affirmation of the transcendent unicity of God, which coexists with some religious forms that admit polygamy, such as Islam and the patriarchal Mormons. Rather, what is referred to here is monotheism as it has been manifested in Judeo-Christian salvation history, which by degrees the divine love revealed as characteristic of an elective and personal preference, ever more characterized by exclusivity and the definiteness of an indissoluble pact. The God of Israel is the God who enters into an exclusive covenant with his people. It implies a relationship of reciprocal belonging ("I am your God and you are my people" is the formula of the covenant, cf. *Ez* 19-20) and promises fidelity without reserve. He is a jealous God, but is always capable of pardoning after betrayals, because he is faithful to himself and the word given is given once and for all.

So, little by little, in the history of salvation narrated by the Sacred Scriptures, the relationship of the covenant is expressed with the metaphor of the bridegroom of the wedding.[137] God's agape does

---

[136] In this respect, see: J. Noriega, *El destino del eros. Perspectivas de moral sexual*, Calabra, Madrid 2004.

[137] The title alone is indicative: in this respect, see among a vast amount of literature: L. Alonso Schökel, *I nomi dell'amore. Simboli matrimoniali nella Bibbia*, Piemme, Casale M. 1997; on the topic of God´s jealousy: D. Barthelemy, *Dio e la sua immagine*, Jaca Book, Milano 1975; A. Sicari, *Matrimonio e verginitá nella rivelazione. L'uomo di fronte alla "Gelosia di Dio"*, Jaca Book, Milano 1978.

not fear to assume forms of human eros. So, at the same time, human eros is revealed in its ultimate tension, purified of dross and imperfections and ennobled in the extreme. The exchange in the analogy cited earlier is verified in just this manner: God has assumed the modalities expressive of spousal love, the point of reference (*analogatum princeps*), so as to understand that what is truly love now is not the human love between man and woman; it is divine love. This love is personal, exclusive with respect to a person, faithful and definitive. Only monogamy can truly reflect the divine likeness of the love of the one God. Despite the fact that God may have accepted polygamy and divorce by condescension to human weakness and infidelity, it was not so in the beginning: his original plan, definitively revealed by Jesus, is one of a marriage that is unique and indissoluble (cf. *Mt* 19:3-9).

Precisely in Jesus the definitive event of God's love for his people is realized. He is the Spouse. With Jesus, the initial design for human love in the divine plan is manifested, not as a law so rigorous that it is impracticable on account of the weakness of the human condition but as an ultimate communication of love, which becomes a redemption and a new possibility for human love. On the Cross, he has given himself totally and from his opened side blood and water flows, the sign of baptism and the Eucharist, the sacraments which give birth to and nourish the Church. The Fathers saw in this event the birth of the new Eve, the Church, which comes forth from the wounded side of the sleeping Spouse, the new Adam. Jesus, on the cross, reveals the ultimate meaning of love with the fruitful gift of himself, which continually regenerates in forgiveness the possibility of loving a human spouse. St Ignatius of Antioch wrote to the Romans: "My eros is crucified", demonstrating in this way the transfiguration of human love that Christ achieves in the crucible of divine agape.[138] The water of the human love between man and woman is transformed into the wine of God's love which flows superabundantly, is better than the

[138] St Ignatius of Antioch, *Letter to the Romans*, VII, 2 ; in this respect: M. Tenace, "Il mio eros è crocifisso: la sapienza della croce", in J.-J. Pérez-Soba – L. Granados, (Ed.), *Il Logos dell'agape. Amore e ragione come principi dell'agire*, Lateran University Press, Roma 2008 (in process of publication).

first, and is placed at the disposal of human spouses.

As the title of the first part of the Encyclical indicates, there emerges in Christ "the unity of love in creation and in the history of salvation. Creation itself must be understood as an act of original love, laying the premises for overcoming the merely appetitive dynamic of eros in a logic of gift.[139] The Christian novelty which attributes to God the capacity of loving made it necessary to open a more extensive meaning to love, which at the same time revealed its uniquely personal value. Consequently, eros can also be understood starting from creation and it manifests in this way an intrinsic orientation to its being completed in that gift of self in which agape is realized. From the theological point of view, the contraposition is overcome by means of a Christocentric reading of creation and its gratuitous destination in the fullness of charity. We are not concerned here with a mechanical identity based on nature, but with a dynamic unity achieved by the gift of grace and man's freely-being-disposed to it. The possibility of love as agape is always dependent on the original love of God being manifested and communicated and on man's acceptance of this prior gift through faith.

The analogical character of love also becomes clear here. This implies a radical distinction between an original creative love and an appetitive love proper to creatures which responds by nature to the love which precedes it. To recognize the essential difference between the original love of God and the love proper to creatures prevents this last becoming absolute, thereby attributing to it a creative value disconnected from any reference to appetite. The insurmountable difference opens it, instead, to a synergy which enables it to find fulfilment in the logic of the gift.

---

[139] See: K.L. Schmitz, *The Gift: Creation*, Marquette University Press, Milwaukee 1982; J.-J. Pérez-Soba, "Status quaestionis: l'amore ci fa pensare", in J.-J. Pérez-Soba – L. Granados, (Ed.), *Il Logos dell'agape*, op. cit.

3. Dynamic Integration

But how is eros integrated in agape? How can we realize this road of transformation and purification which allows human love to accommodate divine love?

Firstly, let us begin with a simple answer: when eros is untied from the man-woman archetype and from the nuptial mystery which constitutes its original structure, then eros – the Encyclical records this for us – shows itself to be "...intoxicated and undisciplined", "not an ascent in "ecstasy" towards the Divine, but a fall, a degradation of man. Evidently, *eros* needs to be disciplined and purified if it is to provide not just fleeting pleasure, but a certain foretaste of the pinnacle of our existence, of that beatitude for which our whole being yearns" (*DCE* 4).

In order not to be lost, eros must, therefore, encounter a law and follow a way, which in time fulfills the promise which is enclosed within it from the event of the first encounter. The law is not an end in itself. Its mission is to offer pointers concerning the way, an instruction concerning the kinds of wanting and acting which will fulfill the intuited promise as well as those which, instead, make its realization impossible.[140] But where is this law to be found and what form can it have so that love is not an extrinsic imposition which would suffocate the most profound desires by mortifying their impulse and poisoning their most beautiful moments?

The law presupposes a fundamental behaviour that allows for its acceptance, namely: faith. To love always means *to believe in love* (*DCE* 1), in that love which is gift and which precedes us. The fact of being a dynamic reality which involves the person in a relationship means that love is of itself open to faith, which gives it a horizon and meaning. It concerns a factor that is intrinsic to the very dynamism of love, which forms part of the logic which is proper to it and which enables one to construct a life starting from it.[141] Faith is the recognition of

---

[140] Cf. G. Angelini, *Eros e agape*, op. cit., pp. 67-73.

[141] See: J.-J. Pérez-Soba, "Una nuova apologetica", op. cit., p. 160, which highlights that this is something more than just a demonstration of the credibility of love as the fundamental reason for the awakening of faith.

the original hope of the encounter in the totality of its factors and on that basis it merits to be followed. By believing in love and by drawing near to the other, little by little, one increasingly discovers himself, overcoming the egotistic character that dominates when eros, loosing itself from the experience which determined it, becomes vague and indeterminate. In self surrender, he will care for the other and her happiness as his own law and will integrate the dimension of desire within the oblative dimension: he will be increasingly concerned for the beloved; he will give himself to her and will desire "to be for the other" (cf. *DCE* 7).

The affections develop a decisive role on this road from eros to agape. In a concrete way, they enable the discovery of the values associated with the other, as vital experiences referring to a person. In particular, the great and profound emotions proper to the experience of love accompany and precede the recognition of the unique value of the person who is loved. Affectivity prepares reason and will respectively to recognize and to choose the person in all his or her truth, beyond what is pleasing or useful for the subject. This is the decisive dimension of the virtues, by means of which the spontaneous appetitive dynamism is shaped and orientated toward the good of the person and becomes, in this way, positive energy in favour of a fully human experience of sensual love. By means of the virtues, particularly chastity, the integration of the acting subject is achieved, which overcomes the fragmentation and disintegration of concupiscence so that the personalistic norm now becomes connatural. This requires that the other be affirmed for his or her own sake, that is, to be loved as an end and never solely as a means for attaining one's own advantage.[142]

However, precisely in the dedication of love, the man and woman experience that their own relationship opens them to the transcendent. This is, above all, because they experience the limitation of being unable, despite their good will and their capabilities, to truly secure the good of the other. The asymmetric character of reciprocity can never accomplish everything, not even in the most mature love; it

[142] In this regard: K. Wojtyla, *Love and Responsibility*, Ignatius, San Francisco, 1981.

finds its symbolic expression in the child. This child, being the fruit of the conjugal union, always comes as a surprise, as a guest arriving from afar, and in this way redefines the mystery of the origin and destiny of love. The experience of love enables an understanding that God is not only the origin of love, but also that communion with him is love's ultimate end: only he can fulfill the life of the one we love;[143] only he can satisfy our life. We note then that eros searches for something that it cannot pursue for itself alone. The man-woman difference is revealed to be a sign of the most radical difference between man and God: the first refers us to the second and only there can its configuration be found. The nuptial mystery between man and woman on earth is the footprint of a mystery that orientates us to heaven.

The sacrament of Marriage is the place in which the Spirit of divine love encounters the love between man and woman in order to heal it and to fulfill its aspirations, making it a way toward that communion with God which alone can satisfy the human heart. The breath of God, exhaled on the Cross as the fullness of agape, penetrates the human flesh of spouses: their desires, their drives, their affections, their feelings, and integrates the dynamisms of love so that they can achieve the gift of self and conjugal communion, the image of the union of Christ and his Church. Here, we have not only a redemption of eros, of its fragmentations and its selfish withdrawals goaded by concupiscence, but also its divinization because it is transformed into conjugal charity. John Paul II had already expressed this in *Familiaris consortio:*

> The Spirit which the Lord pours forth gives a new heart, and renders man and woman capable of loving one another as Christ has loved us. Conjugal love reaches that fullness to which it is interiorly ordained, conjugal charity, which is the proper and specific way in which the spouses participate in and are called to live the very charity of Christ who gave Himself on the Cross (*FC* 13).

The conjugal love between man and woman becomes, thanks to

[143] Concerning this topic: J. Noriega, *Eros e agape nella vita coniugale*, Cantagalli, Siena 2008, pp. 30-31.

the presence of the Spirit, a means of salvation and a way of holiness: spouses, by giving themselves reciprocally to each other, simultaneously communicate divine charity which dwells in their human love.

In this way, the archetype of love, that between man and woman, is surpassed precisely by the encounter with its fulfilment in charity. In the analogy of love, such love is the eminent sign of that nuptial mystery which has its principle analogy in divine love. The man-woman difference leads to the still more radical difference between man and God: the union of love to which it invites is the sign of the definitive communion of persons with the Father; its procreative fruitfulness recalls the superabundance and gratuity of the Spirit.

So, in the new economy of salvation inaugurated with the coming of the Kingdom in Jesus, the form of marriage is accompanied by a new state of life, namely: consecrated virginity, which mysteriously anticipates, through the sign of renunciation, the fullness of the wedding feast of the Lamb. The novelty of divine love, which has irrupted on earth in the Son become man, is manifested in a charismatic gift offered to some: the gift of a singular presence of Jesus in an affective immediacy, which becomes a mysterious anticipation of the eschatological fulfilment of every desire. Consecrated virginity is not therefore the negation of eros and of the nuptial mystery but the mysterious anticipation of its fulfilment and, therefore, a testimony to the ultimate meaning of the amorous desire of every man and woman, namely: communion with God.

4
The Analogy of Spousal Love from *Humanae vitae* to *Deus caritas est*

What issues are at stake with the teaching of *Humanae vitae*? At the time of publication, most of its commentators either considered it to be merely a treatment of conjugal morality, a very delicate issue for the life of so many Christian spouses, or they thought it dealt with a problem of social morality connected to birth control and the spectre of overpopulation. Some warned that underlying the main theme of the Montini Encyclical was an ecclesiological question related to the interpretation of the "aggiornamento" with which the epochal significance of the recently celebrated Vatican II was identified. Was it finally possible to break with a normative tradition that, according to some, appeared to reflect a millenarian undervaluation of sexuality in the Christian milieu?

The pastoral and doctrinal journey of the pontifical Magisterium in the succeeding years, developed in sharp distinction from a cultural environment marked by radical transformations of custom and mentality, indicates that the issues in stake cannot be restricted to the sphere of sexual or social morality. Although this was the focal point of the teaching, *Humanae vitae* in its entirety has been a neuralgic point of contention for many, even for the understanding of the faith itself.[144]

In this chapter, I would like to retrace the journey from Pope Paul VI´s prophecy in *Humanae vitae* to the theological meditation on agape

[144] In this sense, the attempts to re-dimension the extension of the pontifical document and the dissent which followed it have shown themselves to be short-sighted. See, as an example, the attempt of F. Böckle, "*Humanae vitae* als Prüfstein des wahren Glaubens? Zur kirchenpolitischen Dimension moraltheologischer Fragen", in *Stimmen der Zeit* 115 (1990), 3-16.

of *Deus caritas est,* passing through the theology of the body proposed by John Paul II. In this way, the complete panorama of the theology of love will become clear and in its light, the teaching of the Montini Encyclical will be fully comprehensible.

The prophecy of Humanae vitae

The heart of the teaching of *Humane vitae* is found in paragraph 12 where "the inseparable connection (*indissolubilis nexus*) established by God – and which man on his own initiative may not break – between the unitive and procreative meanings inherent to the marriage act" is affirmed.[145] As we can see by this formulation and from the context of the paragraph, the doctrinal foundation of the ethical norm is established on the personalistic value of the conjugal act, not just at the level of physiology. In fact, it concerns that sense of "true and mutual love" and "its ordering to the person's most sublime vocation to parenthood", which has been inscribed in the very being of man and woman by the Creator. This principle is so "profoundly reasonable and human", that Pope Paul VI was confident that it would be at least comprehensible to the contemporary person.

The Montini Encyclical is intended, therefore, to be an argument in favour of the personalistic dignity of conjugal sexuality and of human procreation, both of which can support an integral understanding of love only if they respect the intimate connection between the unity of bodies in the flesh and openness to the transmission of life. Indeed, when intentionally separated from procreation, human sexuality loses its meaning as an integral gift of self full receptivity to the other. Contraception injects into the bodily act of the reciprocal donation between man and woman the poison of a lie, which falsifies it from within, rendering it a self-giving devoid of the gift of self, a receptivity

[145] Among the many theological comments that affirm it, one that is particularly authoritative, coming as it does from the personal theological advisor to Paul VI, who would have had an important role in the preparation of the document, is that of C. Colombo, *L'insegnamento fondamentale di Humanae vitae*, Milano 1989, 411-412.

without hospitality. Indeed, it can be said that a contraceptive act is no longer a conjugal act: in its intentional, objective structure, it fails to recognize the distinct form of conjugal sexual activity, obtaining only an individualistic and hedonistic satisfaction which is incapable of constructing a real, personal communion.

On the other hand, procreation which is not derived from a sexual, conjugal act takes on board the characteristics of a technical-productive activity, regulated by the logic of an efficacy of means in relation to the intended results in which the personal dignity of the child is no longer respected. The child is no longer received as a gift that comes from a gift but is instead programmed and produced as an object, over which one can always exercise the power of verification concerning the initial plan. So one could say that the doctrine of *Humanae vitae* represents the "formulation of the conditions according to which conjugal sexuality is able to express true love. It is a defence of sexuality as the true expression of spousal and personal love"[146] and, at the same time, the defense of the personalistic dimension of human procreation.

It is interesting to note that the teaching of *Humanae vitae* is given precisely at the dawn of that vast and complex cultural phenomenon that goes by the name of "sexual revolution" and which has extended its influence into the modern milieu by means of a widespread eroticism. The prophetic character of the Encyclical fully emerges precisely in this light. It expresses a judgement that is both timely and dramatically pertinent with respect to a cultural revolution whose radical and subversive character is only now being fully recognized.

The sexual revolution[147] is the programmatic attempt to separate the sexual activity from the institution of marriage and from the perspective of paternity and maternity. The vast diffusion of contraception makes possible the claim that sexuality has been freed

[146] Cf. M. Rhonheimer, *Sexualität und Verantwortung. Empfängnisverhütung als ethisches Problem*, Imabe, Wien 1995, 63.

[147] The ideological point of reference is the work of W. Reich, *La rivoluzione sessuale*, Feltrinelli, Milano 1963 (orig. German: 1936); for a description of the phenomenon, see F. Giardini, *La rivoluzione sessuale*, Edizioni Paoline, Roma 1974.

from its institutional or permanent ties. Separated from its natural and traditional bonds, within which its meaning was found, the exercise of sexuality assumes "libido" as a single point of reference and the satisfaction of its desire as the sole criterion of verification.

In this way, sexuality is also separated from the sexual differentiation between man and woman: from the moment that "gender" is understood as a cultural construct and therefore an object of an individual choice, it is no longer necessary that natural sex be a binding point of reference. "Plastic" sexuality, freed from any link to procreation, becomes individualistic: in democratic society, we can observe a drive toward an epochal transformation of intimacy.[148] Love and sexuality tend to be no longer linked to marriage; rather, by means of "pure relationships", in the sense of social relationships which prescind from every form predetermined by nature or by culture, they depend only on the calculation of advantages and disadvantages from which either party can withdraw.

Far from bringing about authentic freedom, the sexual revolution seems to have provoked instead an extraordinary obsession with sex. This seemingly pervasive phenomenon is difficult to define and has been described as "pansexualism".[149] It concerns a cultural proposal that reduces sexuality to genitality and considers it to be a mere object of consumption, the enjoyment of which, on the part of the individual, is normal and good. It is an attempt to radically secularize sexuality, despoiling it of all mystery and transcendence, including its most interior longing: the desire to build a communion of persons. Instead, it becomes a mere occasion of pleasure.[150] However, the search for pleasure as an end in itself, deprives sexuality of the most secret promise which animates it and renders it so fascinating. The obsession with sexuality is the final consequence of a hedonism which in the end destroys even the capacity for achieving pleasure.

[148] Cf. A. Giddens, *The Transformation of Intimacy: sexuality, love and eroticism in modern societies,* Stanford University Press, CA, USA, 1993.

[149] J.-J. Pérez-Soba Diez del Corral, "El pansexualismo de la cultura actual", in *El corazón de la familia, Presencia y dialogo*, Madrid 2006, 339-376. *Anthropotes* XX/1 (2004) was also dedicated to the topic of pansexualism.

[150] Cf. J. Noriega, *Il destino dell'eros. Prospettive di morale sessuale*, EDB, Bologna 2006.

The prophetic character of *Humanae vitae* consists precisely in having hit upon the crucial point of the phenomenon of socio-cultural transformation, so significant in our time. In going against the tide with respect to the prevailing mentality, the Encyclical of Paul VI affirmed the capital importance of that vision of sexuality according to which it is a true expression of love and a personal, integral gift, capable of constructing an authentic communion and open to life. As I will now try to demonstrate, the magisterium of the Church, in the years that followed, with John Paul II and Benedict XVI, has developed the potentialities of this prophecy, documenting it in an ever richer and increasingly articulated theology of love.

The analogy of love in John Paul II: perichoresis with the anthropological question

It has been rightly observed that John Paul II, in his extensive magisterial teaching on the topic, particularly in the remarkable cycle of Wednesday Catecheses of the first years of his pontificate, established an intimate connection and something of a perichoresis between the matrimonial and the anthropological questions.[151] In other words: where conjugal love is concerned, man himself is at stake, as is a true anthropological understanding of love.

This thesis, developed precisely in reference to *Humanae vitae,* was established through the elaboration of a truly significant "theology of the body", in which he exposed, for the first time and in an organic way, the vision of human corporeity which springs from revelation, considered in the light of the original human experiences. The human body, marked by the sexual difference, is the "sacrament of the person": the visible sign of the invisible reality that constitutes

[151] This statement comes from C. Caffarra, *Prefazione*, a Giovanni Paolo II, *Familia via Ecclesiae. Il Magistero di Papa Wojtyla sul matrimonio e la famiglia*, Ed. G. Grandis, Cantagalli, Siena 2006, 7-16. The Wednesday Catecheses are collected in: John Paul II, *Uomo e donna lo creò. Catechesi sull'amore umano*, Città Nuova – Libreria Editrice Vaticana, Roma 1985. Renowned for its critical rigor and its introduction, see the recent English edition: *Man and Woman He Created Them. A Theology of the Body.* Translation, Introduction, and Index by Michael Waldstein, Pauline, Boston 2006.

us as unique and unrepeatable subjects.[152] Far from being reduced to its physiological dimension, a tendency of the empirical sciences, the body is permeated by subjectivity. It is in the body that man discovers his irreducible difference from other living beings and so experiences, in the visible world, his original solitude and, at the same time, his call to communion in the encounter with the body-person of the woman. Precisely in this way, the possibility of a unique experience of intimacy and a unique reciprocity is revealed to him: the body manifests its nuptial meaning. Therefore, the gestures of the body must be understood in terms of the call to express a language which achieves a loving communion of persons and in which nature and person are indissolubly interwoven.[153]

The positive significance of human sexuality and the dignity of man now appear in full light. He is the subject of love precisely in the unity of body and soul which constitutes him.[154] In this sense, the meaning of the body calls him to the gift of self and receptivity to the other. Self-mastery is the condition for the full realization of this vocation and it is achieved by means of the virtues, particularly the virtue of chastity. This latter must be understood, not as a repression of the passions and of affectivity, but rather as the virtue of true love: the interior strength that allows the urges and emotions to express themselves with full respect for the personal dignity of the other, achieving an authentic communion of persons in the act of conjugal love.

The newness of language and of approach to the topic of sexuality provoked a great clamor of public opinion. It was indeed considered to be a radical overcoming of that puritanical suspicion which had for centuries imprisoned Catholic sexual morality in a false and reductive interpretation. Puritanism consists in a deformation of the very

---

[152] Op. cit, *Man and Woman He Created Them. A Theology of the Body*, TOB 29; 87. See also in this regard: J. Merecki, "Il corpo, sacramento della persona", in L. Melina – S. Grygiel (Eds), *Amare l'amore umano*, cit., pp. 173-185.

[153] Op. cit., *Man and Woman He Created Them*, TOB 103, p. 531.

[154] Cf. G. Marengo, "Legge naturale, corpo e libertà", in L. Melina - J. Noriega (Eds), *Camminare nella luce. Prospettive della teologia morale a partire da "Veritatis splendor"*, Lateran University Press, Roma 2004, 631-641.

content of Christianity; it had originated in the Protestant environment and can be expressed in the following series of equations: "God" is equivalent to "morality"; "morality" is equivalent to a series of "prohibitions"; "prohibitions" refer above all to "sexuality".[155] In this way, the assertion of God becomes equivalent to sexual repression.

Nietzsche's accusation against Christianity, recalled by Pope Benedict XVI in his inaugural encyclical, can therefore be understood in this light: according to Nietzsche, Christianity poisoned *eros*, turning to bitterness the most beautiful thing in life.[156] However, the Catecheses of John Paul II catch such prejudices and accusations off guard and open the way to a rediscovery of the value of the body in Christianity, a theme particularly dear to the Fathers of the Asiatic tradition.[157] As has been observed: "with John Paul II, it was suddenly beautiful to be Christian", precisely because one could see the goodness and the harmony in the deepest desires of the human heart.

At the same time, however, the spiritualistic misunderstanding implied in some personalisms and at variance with the personalism of *Humanae vitae* was also overcome.[158] Indeed, according to this misunderstanding, the evaluation of the interpersonal relationship of love, understood as the "primary end" of the conjugal act, had been reduced to the "procreative end", in this way levelling and even flattening it to a biologistic vision. In reality, the perspective of John Paul II's theology of the body, while clearly highlighting the personalistic dignity of the conjugal act, recognizes the inner meaning of the gift of self in the spouses' openness to fruitfulness, something that cannot be willfully excluded without undermining the integral value of the act itself. The intimate and indissoluble unity of three factors is manifested here; these factors constitute what has been called the "nuptial mystery": sexual difference, unity in the flesh and

[155] J.-J. Pérez-Soba Diez del Corral, *El corazón de la familia*, cit., 352-354.

[156] Benedict XVI, Enc. *Deus caritas est*, n. 3.

[157] Cf. J. Granados, *Los misterios de la vida de Cristo en Justino Mártir*, « Analecta Gregoriana », Ed. Pug, Roma 2005; «You are the Light of the World ». Mission of the Family, Small Domestic Church", in *Anthropotes* XXIII/2 (2007), in course of publication.

[158] Cf. G. Mazzocato, "Il dibattito tra Doms e neotomisti sull'indirizzo personalista", in *Teologia* 31 (2006), 249-275.

fecundity.[159]

The term "mystery" ultimately suggests an opening to something beyond; it does not indicate, according to a rationalistic interpretation, something that remains obscure and unknowable to reason, but something that, however much it is revealed, remains in itself beyond the possibilities of reason's comprehension. It is revealed in the modality of the sign. But in what sense is the experience of human love a mediation for an analogical reference to God? How is it a way by which we can come to know God the Creator?

In the act of love we will always find reference to a lover and to a beloved. Together, these constitute a final and insuperable point of reference, according to which the person is loved for his or her own sake. Nevertheless, the dynamism of love, which is orientated to the person, is itself part of a preceding causality which surpasses it.[160] We are referring to an act of original love which envelops the whole of Creation and points to its radical goodness, according to which it is worthy of being loved. This leads us to recognize that human love is preceded by an original, creative love in such a way that the latter is manifested in the former and renders it possible. It is precisely this presence of the love of God the Creator in every act of human love that allows for the analogy of love: starting from the experience of love, a way of knowing God is opened which has a particular characteristic: that is, it summons human freedom to account concerning its availability to love as a necessary condition of the cognitive act.

The way of charity in Benedict XVI: perichoresis with the theological question

The teaching of Pope Benedict XVI begins here. He develops a profound theology of love, to which he dedicates the inaugural

[159] Cf. A. Scola, *Il mistero nuziale. 1. Uomo-Donna*, Pul-Mursia, Roma 1998 (*The Nuptial Mystery*, Eerdmans, Michigan2005); *2. Matrimonio-Famiglia*, Pul-Mursia, Roma 2000.

[160] Cf. L. Melina - J. Noriega - J.J. Pérez-Soba, *Camminare nella luce dell'amore. I fondamenti della morale cristiana*, Cantagalli, Siena 2008, 125-127.

encyclical of his pontificate. Love constitutes the very centre of the Christian message: "God is love": he is not concerned with a philosophical idea, but with the adhesion of faith to a historical event: "So we know and believe the love God has for us" (*1 Jn* 4:16). In fact, "Being Christian is not the result of an ethical choice or a lofty idea, but the encounter with an event, a person, which gives life a new horizon and a decisive direction".[161] What characterizes this latest stage of the Magisterium is its emphasis on the intimate connection between the question of love and theological enquiry, as well as the catalogical method of the reflection.

The Pope follows a pointer of St Augustine which remains equally valid today. The great Father of the Church, responding to Psalm 41, with its disquieting question: "men say to me continually, "Where is your God?", says, "If you see love, you see the Trinity".[162] The visibility of the intimate mystery of the one and triune God is made possible by charity, which is realized in the Church. In this way, the question of an authentic love, animated by a charity infused by the Holy Spirit, acquires the value of a divine testimony, above all in a world in which a spiritual blindness in the face of Creation is both dramatic and pervasive while an intellectual blindness toward others puts the existence of God to the test.

Human action, insofar as it welcomes the Divine Spirit, initiates charity and represents a unique testimony to God, a true epiphany of his glory among men.[163] In particular, Christian marriage and family are clothed with a permanent sacramental meaning for the world: precisely by achieving an authentic communion of persons in charity, they are called to testify to God's salvific presence. Indeed, among the multiplicity of meanings of the word love, "one in particular

---

[161] Benedict XVI, Enc. *Deus caritas est*, n. 1. Cf. L. Melina – C. Anderson (Eds), *La via dell'amore. Riflessioni sull'enciclica* Deus caritas est *di Benedetto XVI*, Pontifical John Paul II Institute for Studies on Marriage and Family – Rai Eri, Roma 2006.

[162] St Augustine, *De Trinitate*, VIII, 8, 12.14. See also: J. Granados: «"Vides Trinitatem, si caritatem vides": via del amor y Espiritu Santo en el "De Trinitate" de San Augustin», in *Revista Augustiniana* 43/130 (2002), 23-62.

[163] Allow me to refer you to my volume: L. Melina, *Azione: epifania dell'amore. La morale cristiana oltre il moralismo e l'antimoralismo*, Cantagalli, Siena 2008.

stands out: love between man and woman, where body and soul are inseparably joined and human beings glimpse an apparently irresistible promise of happiness".[164]

This implies that the transparency of the archetype is the necessary condition for being able to access the knowledge of original love. The divine image in man is realized precisely when he, in love, expresses the communion of persons, united in the fruitful gift of themselves. The *analogy* of love (*ανά λόγος*: a pronouncement which starts from below) points to the likeness in an ever greater degree of unlikeness: human love grants access to the divine love which precedes it and is offered to it as a light and strength for self-realization according to truth.

At the same time, it is the *catalogia* (*κατά λόγος*: a pronouncement that descends from above) of the revelation of Trinitarian love in Christ that unveils to man the ultimate meaning of human love itself: in the symbolism of the love of Christ the Bridegroom for the Church, his Bride, the value of conjugal love as a sacrament is manifested. Let us take up again here a second key statement of the encyclical of Pope Benedict: "Corresponding to the image of a monotheistic God is monogamous marriage". The revelation of God in the history of Israel, which culminates in Jesus Christ, the Son of God, manifests the definitive dimension of love and, at the same time, opens to man the possibility of achieving the original plan of God. "God's way of loving becomes the measure of human love".[165] The anthropological truth of conjugal love, which in its original structure is constituted by the threefold dimension of sexual difference, the gift of self and procreation, is the created icon of the divine, Trinitarian love.[166]

The light which descends from above enables a new knowledge within the same ambit of love. It is the way of charity, that "most

---

[164] Enc. *Deus caritas est*, n. 2.

[165] Ibid., n. 11.

[166] A. Scola, "Il mistero nuziale. Originarietà e fecondità", in *Anthropotes* XXIII/2 (2007), in course of publication. For a more systematic treatment, two other volumes by the same author of the work cited here can be seen: *Il mistero nuziale: una prospettiva di teologia sistematica*, Lateran University Press, Roma 2003. (See in English: *The Nuptial Mystery*, Eerdmans, Michigan, 2005).

excellent way of all" (*1 Cor* 12:32), which St Paul has described in his famous hymn of chapter 13 of his First Letter to the Corinthians. Through that way, it is possible to arrive at a "love that has no end", that is, at a reality of which we do not yet have direct experience, but without which any experience of love is shown to be inconsistent and ultimately false. Love, as a process of ascent toward God, made possible by the charity of Him who first descended to us, is a progressive light of knowledge. In it, the subject is personally involved, through knowledge, with his freedom: indeed, the truth of which we are now speaking cannot be seen from just an external perspective but is manifested when it is played out in love. "He who does what is true comes to the light" (*Jn* 3:21). Every dualism between faith and morality is therefore excluded: it is in the practical dynamism of love that the truth is manifested.

In this way, the perichoresis between the act of faith in divine revelation and the concrete practice of love, and more specifically that of conjugal love in its truth, is perceived still more clearly in the interior unity of the Christian event. The human love between man and woman finds its truth, its language and its grammar, ultimately founded on God's original plan, to be instituted in Creation and definitively revealed in Jesus Christ. Respect for the inseparable unity between the unitive and procreative meanings of the conjugal act, forms part of the grammar of love, that is, that system of rule which enables authentic communion between persons. "I am afraid that as long as we believe in the grammar, we would continue to believe in God" Friedrich Nietzsche had stated.[167] Certainly, however, as has been recently and shrewdly observed by Robert Spaemann,[168] a grammar was also necessary for Nietzsche in order to write as he wished and even to assert his denial of God. The truth is the inescapable context that intentionally embraces all of our discourses, even the discourses

[167] Cited in L. Irigaray, *Éthique de la différence*, cit., 109; the nietzschian statement is footnoted in *Die "Vernunft" in der Philosophie*, 5. Also in the same sense, Jacques Derida stated that the epoch of meanings is essentially theological and presupposes God (*De la grammatologie*, Minuit, Paris 1967, 41).

[168] R. Spaemann, *Der letzte Gottesbeweis*, Pattloch, München 2007.

of those who try to deny that it is ultimately based on God. The grammar of love has its source in God the Creator and Redeemer: do deny it is to obscure his face.

Conclusion

What is it that is ultimately at stake with *Humanae vitae*? This is the question that we began with. Our rapid perusal of the development of theological thought, tied to the magisterium of John Paul II and Benedict XVI, has shown that it is not just a norm of sexual morality that is at stake which could effectively be put aside, bypassed or easily changed in the future. It has become clear that the anthropological and theological questions are tied to the question of marital sexuality, precisely because all of these main themes are tied to love. Once more the interior, organic unity of Catholic truth has been demonstrated. In the truth, the whole is always implied in the fragment which in turn draws its meaning from the whole to which it essentially contributes. For this reason, it is never possible to separate the truth of God from the truth of man, or the faith as believed from the faith as practised in daily life.

The rupture of the intimate nexus between sexuality and one's openness to procreation is the expression of a process of a radical secularization of human love which is progressively reduced to the utilitarian and individualistic dimension of a search for one's own pleasure. It is a search which, embarked upon in this way, increasingly lead to a frustration of desire, even to the point of impoverishing pleasure. So, the defence of love as "mystery" is, at the same time, a defence of God and of man. Ultimately, it is also a defence of desire and of the human joys of sexuality.

Therefore, the integral preaching of the truth of human love, taught by *Humanae vitae*, is an integral part of evangelization and of the task of constructing an authentic civilization of love and a culture of the family.[169] The Church does not teach these truths because she is obsessed with sexuality; if she goes against the tide, it is not in order to repress but rather to collaborate with the authentic joy of men and women, pointing them along the way of love.

[169] See in this regard: C. Anderson, *A Civilization of Love. What Every Catholic Can Do to Transform the World*, Harper One, New York 2008; L. Melina, *Per una cultura della famiglia. Il linguaggio dell'amore*, Marcianum, Venezia 2006.

5
The Gift that enables us to Hope: Benedict XVI's Spe salvi and Vatican II's Gaudium et spes

"He who offers the greatest hope conquers the world", said Father Luigi Giussani. Indeed, there is nothing more necessary to men's lives than this extraordinary little virtue. It is a virtue, Charles Péguy observed, that astonishes even God, so humanly implausible is it. "That poor children, seeing how things are, believe that they will improve – they see how things are today and believe that tomorrow they will be better – this is truly astonishing and a great marvel of grace."[170] Neither faith nor charity surprise God: faith is a faithful wife, charity a mother; he is certainly astonished, however, by hope: hope is like a little baby, a helpless child, but it is precisely this little one who moves the world. God, in fact, never works except through children. "Hanging by the arms between her two older sisters who hold her hands, little hope moves forward. Being in the middle, it seems as though hope is being led. In reality, it is hope that enables the other two to walk". What then will the relationship between hope and love turn out to be? The answer to this provides the theme of our present study.

1. The crisis of hope in the postmodern age

Hope needs to be firmly established, because still worse than the lack of hope is the despair that follows bitter delusion. This seems

[170] Ch. Péguy, *Le Porche du mystère de la deuxième vertu*, Gallimard, Paris 1986, p. 20. (In English, *Portal of the Mystery of Hope*, Ressourcement Books, Eerdmans, Cambridge).

to be our spiritual situation. The age in which we live is sometimes described as "post-modern", having experienced the tragedies and horrors of the ideologies and utopias of modernity, which promised a radiant future and a definitive liberation from every form of slavery and misery. It now finds itself bewildered and without the strength to hope. The old Europe, the "land of sunset", is particularly affected by this malady of the heart, the most disquieting symptom of which is the demographic winter into which it has fallen.

Is there any doubt that unemployment and the economic slowdown can be traced to the fact that there are fewer children being born? Basically, this was the diagnosis of John Paul II in the Apostolic Exhortation *Ecclesia in Europa* (n. 7-9) where he spoke of the "dimming of hope", of a "time of bewilderment" and of a "fear of the future". The signs? Beyond the dramatic decrease in birth rate, we can note: an inability of the young to make definitive life choices and an egocentric individualism that leads to suspicion of the other and introspective self-withdrawal. The causes? The loss of historical memory, the lack of roots and, above all, the silent apostasy that simply lives "as though God does not exist". If it is not "disperato" (desperate – from the Italian di + sperare = without hope), our world is at least "di-speranzato", that is, in the process of being sapped of hope.[171]

Paradoxically, the revolution of 1968 seemed at the time to be an opening and an opportunity for Europe. The banner of hope was raised, or at least its reinterpretation, rendering hope immanent to history. Ernst Bloch's *Daz Prinzip Hoffnung* attempted to provide a theological dimension to the revolutionary impetus of Marxism in the religious élan of a secularized eschatology: hope must be the principle that tows the world forward, by anticipating what does not yet exist.[172] Optimism is for him the expression of the new faith in history, in which God is substituted by revolutionary activity. The

[171] The play on words is lost in English – the original Italian text reads: "Se non disperato, il nostro mondo è almeno 'di-speranzato'."

[172] See in this regard: J. Ratzinger, *The Yes of Jesus Christ, Spiritual Exercises in Faith, Hope and Love,* Crossroad, NY, 1991, 41-43.

German thinker elaborated, therefore, an ontology of the not (yet) existing in which hope is a virtue of struggle, a force that pushes on in the march toward utopia. Indeed, fifty years after this proclamation and forty years from its response in the student revolutions, very little of Bloch's optimism actually remains in the conscious experience of our postmodern generation. Ideological optimism, the ephemeral surrogate of Judeo-Christian hope, very quickly exhausted the supply of propellant and the rocket which was to have been triumphantly launched to the stars of the future, drawing humanity to the new world, is now parked in a hangar in a forlorn state of disrepair. What exhausted the fuel supply, leading to a dissipation of energy and impetus, and to the current spiritual breakdown?

Spe Salvi **and** Gaudium et Spes: **an intriguing question**

It is precisely this situation which concerns Benedict XVI in his second encyclical, *Spe salvi.* Faced with the question, "in what can we place our hope?" (n. 1), he proposes a twofold self-critique as a necessary preliminary, namely: a self-critique of the modern age in dialogue with Christianity; a self-critique of modern Christianity itself, which has been incapable of "giving reasons for hope" (*1 Pet* 3:15) and has even reduced and hidden it, thus depriving the world of the necessary light that only Christians possess. In fact, hope is the element that chiefly distinguishes Christian men and women: they have a future because they have God. In comparison with the pagans who had many gods, but did not have God in the world, and so were without hope, the first Christians were identified precisely by their hope (cf. *Ef* 2:12; *1 Tim* 4:13). Pope Benedict, however, radically and concretely poses the question: "is Christian faith, even for us today, a hope that transforms and sustains our life?" (n. 10).

It has been mischievously observed that in the Pope's document, for the first time in a recent pontifical text, there is no reference to Vatican II, and particularly to the pastoral constitution *Gaudium et spes.* Among the conciliar documents this one has been explicitly understood to institute a dialogue with the people of our time, precisely on the subject of hope. Let us recall the opening words: "The joys and the hopes, the griefs and the anxieties of the men of this age, especially those who are poor or in any way afflicted, these are the joys and hopes, the griefs and anxieties of the followers of Christ. Indeed, nothing genuinely human fails to raise an echo in their hearts". Indeed, could it be that the self-criticism that Benedict XVI hopes for, even within Christianity, would even include the Second Vatican Council or at least that widespread, naive and optimistic reading of it in relation to history, which would have Christianity flattened to the level of the modern ideology of progress?[173]

The intriguing question of the relationship between *Spe salvi* and *Gaudium et spes* leads us to a reading of Pope Benedict's second encyclical which primarily sees in it some clear guidelines for a self-criticism of modern Christian thought concerning hope, also in reference to a critical reading of modernity; starting with this, it will be possible to positively retrace the integral dimensions of Christian hope, to which Christianity must bear witness in the world, so that people can walk with certainty of the future.

2. Critique of individualism and the communitarian dimension of Christian salvation

The first self-criticism that we find in the pontifical text concerns the individualistic reduction of Christian hope which can be observed even from the dawn of the modern era. The Pope explicitly quotes here the 1938 work of Henri de Lubac, namely, *Catholicisme. Aspects sociaux du dogme (Catholicism: Social Aspects of Dogma),* in which the great French theologian reproposes the communitarian dimensions of Christian salvation.

In relation to modern man who accepts the world and through science has come to know the laws for transforming it, ultimately,

[173] This is the interpretation of the encyclical offered by A. Socci, "Che cosa significa la bellissima enciclica di Benedetto XVI sulla speranza", in *Libero* 1st December, 2007.

into the kingdom of man on earth, the Christian man or woman is seen as one who withdraws from the city of men and is concerned only for the salvation of his own soul.[174] The Christian's great hope is, in this way, estranged from the world and from the history of humanity: it is reduced to the subjective and ineffable interiority of the individual soul and, at the same time, delayed until the next world. Christianity is reduced to spiritualism, to a flight from the real world of affectivity and work, from society and from politics. Faced with the invasive attack of modern scientific rationality, it has tried to save itself by fleeing into the private sphere, but precisely in this way has condemned itself to insignificance. However, the price to be paid for a merely provisional survival is simply too high.

The path indicated by de Lubac, along which we are escorted by the Fathers of the Church, is instead one of rediscovering the original dimensions of the Christian assertion, namely: an integral salvation, which involves, not only his soul but man's body and history, and not just the individual's salvation but the salvation of the community, the culture and all humanity as the great family of the children of God: "the new heavens and the new earth". The Gospel indeed proclaims the Incarnation of the Son of God, his true resurrection in the flesh and the primacy of a new creation which embraces all reality anticipated in the sign of a communion of persons in the mystical body of the Church.

Pope Benedict is concerned to point out that the indispensible condition for such a recovery of the integrity of Christian salvation is "reason's openness to the saving forces of faith, to the differentiation between good and evil. Only thus does reason become truly human" (n. 23). On another occasion, he counselled the "opening up of the space of rationality to the great questions of the true and the good, in this way uniting theology, philosophy and the sciences, with full respect for their own methods and autonomy, but also conscious of

---

[174] Cf. H. de Lubac, *Cattolicismo. Aspetti sociali del dogma*, "Opera omnia" vol. VII, Jaca Book, Milano 1978, p. XXII.

their intrinsic unity together."[175]

The exclusion from the field of knowledge of everything that transcends the empirically experiential has lead to a mechanistic and materialistic view of the world, which renders it manipulable at will. The realization of the astonishing possibilities opened by technology has nevertheless been accompanied in recent times by an ever more acute perception of its risks, in terms of the ecological destruction of the planet and the arbitrary and disturbing manipulations on the part of anonymous and unchecked power. Here we recognize aspects of reality that are disregarded and misunderstood: the world is not just material for indiscriminate action. It bear within itself a "logos" to be recognized and respected. The rationality of the sciences must be subject to the rationality of a more comprehensive knowing and be capable of harmonizing with the meanings that the Logos of the Creator has inscribed in creation. Only in this way can an ideology of progress that claims to achieve man's hope in mechanistic and automatic terms be overcome: "It is not science that redeems man. Man is redeemed by love" (n. 26).

We can note a surprising coincidence at this point between *Spe salvi* and the letter and spirit of *Gaudium et spes* which from n. 24 to n. 30 is aimed at illustrating "the communitarian nature of the human vocation in the plan of God", the social characteristics of the human being and the importance of the common good, all of which point to the need to overcome a purely individualistic ethics. The most original aspect of Benedict XVI's discourse is his critique of scientific ideology as an automatic driver of progress. So, we could say that *Spe salvi* simply develops, in a profoundly changed context, the fundamental intention of the Second Vatican Council, expressing, in a way that is more mindful of the threats and risks, a cultural critique of scientific unilateralism. However, another crucial question arises in this regard, namely: what is the relationship between Christian hope and humanity's hope for the historical betterment of his world?

---

[175] Benedict XVI, *Discorso ai partecipanti al IV Convegno Nazionale della Chiesa Italiana*, Verona, cit.. The invitation had been extended so as to here again from the Pope his famous *Address at the University of Regensburg* on the 12th September, 2006.

3. Critique of immanentism and the transcendent nature of Christian hope

So we have arrived at the second great self-criticism which the encyclical proposes for Christian thought. It concerns the dimensions of Christian hope and its particular content. In effect, the urge to enter into the dynamics of history by aligning oneself with humanity's efforts to transform the world, lead some to yield to the "temptation of reducing the Gospel of salvation to an earthly Gospel".[176] This temptation is yielded to when Christian hope is identified with the immanent hope of a political liberation, even to the extent of subordinating every assertion of faith or theology to the criterion of efficacy in social action in the struggle against oppression.

In order to become "concrete" and "historical", Christian hope has been identified with the political utopia of an ideology, which now becomes the true content of the ideal collective and is pledged to the promotion of man or of his liberation. In effect, this surrender to immanentism assumes two closely related forms, although they can be found to be politically contra-posed. The first is the "liberal" version of faith in the progress of humanity, by means of the boundless development of the technological sciences and the democratic system. The second is the Marxist version, which is aware of the structural contradictions of social relationships and is aimed at a proletarian revolution for securing justice in a new economic, social and political system of radical equality. Both, as the poet, Thomas S. Eliot, wrote "dream of systems so perfect that no one will need to be good. But the man who is will overshadow the man who claims to be".[177] In reality, the failure of both of these immanent utopias has shed light on the ambiguity of progress, which, "without doubt offers new possibilities for the good, but also opens appalling possibilities for evil" (n. 22).

In reality, the great error of Marxism, with its blind faith in scientific

---

[176] Congregation for the Doctrine of the Faith, *Instruction on some aspects of 'Liberation Theology'*, August 6, 1984, VI, 5.

[177] T.S. Eliot, *Cori da 'La Rocca'*, in *Opere*, Bompiani, Milano 1971, pp. 418-419. See also, *Choruses from 'The Rock'*, Rizzoli, 1996.

and social progress, is that of having forgotten that man always remains man; it has forgotten freedom, falling into a mortifying and ultimately oppressive materialism which in the end cannot even assure the economic well-being of the individual (cf. n. 21). Instead, it is clear that "The right state of human affairs...can never be guaranteed through structures alone", because "the kingdom of good will never be definitively established in this world" (n. 24). Man remains free and his freedom is a fragile freedom.

History is then the place of freedom and ethical responsibility for the good and evil of one's own actions. Therefore, it is the place of the patient work of education which can be achieved only where there are witnesses to the good, capable of encouraging and accompanying the freedom of persons.

What is then the specific content of Christian hope? In pages of great spiritual depth, Pope Benedict speaks to us of eternal life, beginning with Jesus' own words in the Gospel of John: "This is the eternal life: that they may know you, the only true God, and him whom you have sent, Jesus Christ" (*Jn* 17:3). Life is always a relationship and the eternal, definitive, fully satisfying relationship is a relationship with Him who is the very source of life (n. 27). In this connection, the Pope proposes once again the truth of faith as presented to the newly baptized: the ultimate eschatological realities of life and history: judgement, hell and heaven. He reproposes here aspects of the content of faith which are frequently omitted in preaching, or presented with a certain embarrassment. Only in the perspective of these realities does human history acquire meaning. Without the resurrection of the dead and without a final judgement, history remains an unsolved and unsoluble enigma because it provides no response to the requirement of justice for the innocent or for the victims of horrendous crimes and abuses. Precisely this deprives the historical commitment to justice of the necessary motivation. In reality, only God can bring about justice and motivate hope: "the question of justice constitutes the strongest argument in favor of eternal life" (n. 43).

It was indeed necessary to recall these ultimate truths. Certainly,

Gaudium et spes had dedicated a paragraph to the topic of the new heavens and the new earth (n. 39) and warned about the danger of identifying earthly progress with the development of the Kingdom of God. So the doctrine is the same. Still, the emphasis of the teaching has changed: in fact, Pope Benedict XVI is addressing the generation of Christian faithful who, in the forty years or so that have passed since the Council, have experienced the disillusionment of the secular utopias and the tragedies they have led to; they have experienced the dangers of identifying Christian hope with objectives that remain immanent to history. He therefore wishes not only to invite Christians to share with all people of good will the task of transforming the world, but also, and above all, that they recognize once again their calling to bear witness to that transcendent content of that great hope, without which even earthly hopes lose their meaning.

4. The paradoxical face of hope and the beatitudes

It is necessary to speak here of the modest and almost hidden face of Christian hope, which has the aspect of a very small and seemingly insignificant seed, recognized and cultivated only by a few. Still, with a very beautiful quotation from St Bernard, the encyclical reminds us that "the human race lives thanks to a few; if it was not for them, the world would perish..." (n. 15).[178] In reality, the smallest seed bears the entire future inside it, just like Jesus' little flock of disciples.

An etymological observation is worth noting here: the word "hope", in its Hebrew root (*qwh – qaw*) has the idea of a "thread", a cord or a rope (e.g. *Joshua* 2: 18-21: the scarlet cord of Rahab, the prostitute). In modern language too, we sometimes speak of holding on to "a thread of hope": hope is a thread that ties the present to the future; to hope is to bind the present to the promised future. The certainty of the future is tied to a present. The medieval symbol of hope is the anchor: we can recall the anchor-cross of the basilica of St

[178] Cf. St Bernard of Clairvaux, *Sententiae* III, 118: CCL 6/2, 215, in which he applies to the monks the teaching of Pseudo-Rufinus.

Clement in Rome. Christ is our hope, because he has been raised and has already penetrated into the heavenly sanctuary. To him our lives can be anchored while we await the fulfilment of the promises already begun (*Heb* 6: 18-20).

The Catechism of the Catholic Church suggests that the virtue of hope corresponds to the desire for happiness inscribed deep in the heart: "Hope is the theological virtue by which we desire the Kingdom of Heaven and the eternal life as our happiness, placing our trust in Christ's promises and relying not on our own strength, but on the help of the grace of the Holy Spirit" (n. 1817). The Italian writer, Cesare Pavese asked, "Has anything been promised us? Then why do we expect so much?" Shall we take the desire for happiness seriously or extinguish it? And how should we act so that the present is not destroyed by the utopia? How can we endure the present with its pervasive denial of hope?

There is a paradox to be faced here. For the Christian, it finds its acute expression in the beatitudes: "Blessed are the poor…blessed are those who mourn…" (*Mt* 5:3ff). What is this about? How can we understand these expressions? Is it not absurd, and a delusion, to imagine that we can sustain the present merely by reference to the future? In reality, Jesus, in his Sermon on the Mount (*Mt* 5-7), which is a proclamation of hope, promises the disciples who follow him a mysterious share in his own destiny: it is he who is the subject of the beatitudes; it is he who is poor, persecuted, meek, etc. He promises the mysterious presence of God and of his Kingdom in the sufferings and contradictions of the present moment. He invites his disciples to live this secret and hidden joy which will one day be fully manifested. The beatitudes are the paradoxical anticipation of the joy of the Kingdom, possible to those who follow the Lord and, in hope, consent to the future promises. Thomas Aquinas refers to the *spes beatitudinis* (hope of beatitude) and to the *beatitudo spei* (beatitude of hope):[179] this is the basis for hope in a future happiness but it is also the foundation of a happiness already begun in the midst of tears and

[179] St Thomas Aquinas, *Summa theologiae*, I-II, 69, 2.

persecutions. The paradox is not a contradiction; it is the Kingdom hidden like a pearl or like a buried treasure.

Here then is the face of one who walks in hope: he is capable both of realism and, at the same time, of inner joy; he is animated by an indefatigable energy. The prophet Isaiah describes his physiognomy in this way: "He (God) gives power to the faint, and to him who has no might he increases strength. Even youths shall faint and be weary, and young men shall fall exhausted; but they who wait for the LORD shall renew their strength, they shall mount up with wings like eagles, they shall run and not be weary, they shall walk and not faint" (*Is* 40:29-31). Hope gives wings; hope flies. Far from promoting passivity, it stimulates extraordinary activity. Bonaventure of Bagnoregio says in an Advent homily: hope demands of us a radical commitment; it demands that we engage our whole being in a movement of opposition to the force of earthly gravity so as to ascend to the sublime height of our being, that is, to the promises of God.[180]

Conclusion

What, then, is hope? Is it possible for us? An ideological optimism of a utopian and political stamp, as Joseph Ratzinger has written,[181] is essentially nothing but a vain attempt to forget death which has as such brought about a "tired and desperate" skepticism.[182] In order to hope, it is necessary to have received a great gift, as Péguy said. The Christian can hope because his present moment has been touched by the future; thanks to the presence of the Lord, he is certain of the future which he awaits and for which he prepares. Hope, as a Christian virtue founded on the Resurrection, is in fact desire which has been saved, both in its original enthusiasm and in the breadth of its expectation, by a gift which is already mysteriously anticipated and

[180] St Bonaventure of Bagnoregio, *Sermo XVI, Dom. I Adv.*

[181] J. Ratzinger, *The Yes of Jesus Christ, Spiritual Exercises in Faith, Hope and Love,* Crossroad, NY, 1991, p. 42.

[182] This pregnant expression comes from Card. Giacomo Biffi, archbishop emeritus of Bologna.

which allows one to hope with patient confidence in the fulfilment of what has been promised us.

So, the relationship between hope and love is now clear: only the original gift of love makes hope possible but, on the other hand, only hope enables one to love.

www.ingramcontent.com/pod-product-compliance
Ingram Content Group UK Ltd.
Pitfield, Milton Keynes, MK11 3LW, UK
UKHW041444070726
13610UKWH00009B/15

9 780852 447789